CONTENTS

To the family who loved baseball first
and nourished my fascination with its numbers:

My mother, Olivia Alanskas, who gave me
my first Strat-O-Matic game;

My father, Alfred Guzzo, who took me
to my first baseball game;

My step-father, Robert Alanskas,
who was always ready to talk baseball;

My uncle, Julius Russu, who in so many ways inspired
my imagination of baseball past and present.

FOREWORD

Baseball is "The National Pastime," and one of the reasons is that there are many different ways to enjoy the game.

Some people are captivated by the pure physical beauty of ballparks—whether in the major or minor leagues, on a college or high school campus, or just at a local park or playground. For example, the first time people see the ivy-covered walls of Wrigley Field—at age three or eighty-three—they are transported to a magical place indeed.

For others, the enjoyment of baseball is in watching one of the greatest games ever invented. The batter-pitcher confrontation is true sport and a competition that happens 50-100 times every game. There is nothing better than the drama of a close play at the plate, the grace of a fielder diving and catching a ball, or the excitement of a runner taking off to steal second base.

And there are always the hot dogs and beer. Nothing tastes better than a true Wisconsin brat and a "genuine" beer at Miller Park in Milwaukee. As Humphrey Bogart said in one of his movies, it beats a steak at the Ritz.

For many of us, it's the numbers of the game that provide our greatest enjoyment. Whether it is just keeping our own scorecard or understanding the nuances of on-base percentage or earned run average, we enjoy baseball because it lends itself to statistical analysis perhaps better than any other human endeavor—or at least any other human endeavor that is so much fun!

◆ ◆ ◆

I have very few memories of my childhood before the age of ten, but my first baseball game stands out, although I don't remember the exact date.

My dad took me to a bat-day doubleheader on the South Side of Chicago. We only lived a few miles from Comiskey Park, where the Chicago White Sox played, and the bat-day doubleheader became an annual tradition for my dad and me. It also became my main source for baseball equipment. Each year's bat was the bat that I used to play "fast-pitching," the version of baseball we played on the South Side. It could be played with as few as two players. A strike-zone box was chalked onto a wall, the pitcher's mound was measured out at a guesstimated distance that seemed fair, and you threw a rubber ball as hard as you could for as long as you could to strike each other out.

For some reason, however, I was drawn to the numbers of baseball from the very first game I ever attended. The best thing I got at the ballpark was the White Sox yearbook. It cost fifty cents back then. I got one every year and sat down and studied the numbers in the book as if it were the Bible: Floyd Robinson was the only Sox player who could hit .300; the ERAs posted by Gary Peters, Joel Horlen, Juan Pizarro and Hoyt Wilhelm were all very, very good (all below 2.50, and usually below 2.00); the all-time single season leader for the White Sox (a tie between Gus Zernial and Ed Robinson) only had 29 home runs. The statistics went on and on. There was no end to them, and every one of them was fascinating to me.

When I was about thirteen years old, I found an ad in *The Sporting News* for a game called Strat-O-Matic Baseball. I walked to the grocery store, bought my money order (remember those?), and sent in my five dollars for the game. A couple of weeks later, after what seemed like an eternity of waiting, the package arrived at my front door. I immediately went over to the schoolyard where my friends were playing a pick-up game of basketball and announced that the game had arrived. The basketball game stopped immediately. We ran to my house and played Strat-O-Matic on my front porch the rest of the summer. I can still see Steve Malkowski running down the street every morning to my house to play the game. I was "Bowie" Dewan that summer, named after Bowie Kuhn, then commissioner of baseball. I was the commissioner of our league, but more importantly, I was the league statistician.

I enjoyed nothing more. I recorded every game I played on scoresheets. When my friends were playing, I recorded their games too. They all had immediate access to their statistics and loved to boast how well Tony Oliva was hitting, or how awesome Bob Gibson was pitching. But our Strat-O-Matic league wasn't enough for me. I began to record stats on my favorite team, the White Sox. I kept day-by-day logs for every player. For this, the daily newspaper was essential. I looked up the boxscores and recorded my logs, one page per player. It got to the point where I spent so much time with my numbers that my mom threatened to take them away. If there was a chore to do and I didn't do it, my stat books were in jeopardy. I even took to hiding them. My favorite place was at the bottom of the laundry hamper, hiding underneath all the clothes waiting to be washed. I'm not sure why I thought my mom would never find them there, since she was the one who washed the clothes! Anyway, once the immediate threat had passed, I'm sure I retrieved my stats before she had a chance to finish the wash.

My love of baseball numbers led directly to my career after graduating from school. I became an actuary, a profession that studies the numbers of insurance. I enjoyed it immensely and was benefiting from a good career. Then I read a book titled *The Bill James Baseball Abstract* in 1982. Bill James was an average guy like me, who loved both baseball and statistics, and he almost single-handedly began the revolution in baseball statistical analysis. Here is my reaction to James' book (as I wrote about in the book *How Bill James Changed Our View of Baseball*):

> A light went on in my head. Here was a guy who was doing with baseball numbers what I had just spent the last six-plus years doing with insurance numbers. I really enjoyed analyzing insurance numbers, but I couldn't believe the same thing could be done with baseball numbers. Sure, the numbers of baseball already existed. In fact, there were already tons of numbers, more than any other sport. A rich tradition of baseball statistics was part of the beauty of the sport. I'd been studying them since I attended my first baseball game in 1963 at the age of eight. James, however, took baseball statistical analysis to a whole new level. He was going deep into the numbers, just as I was doing every day in insurance. But he was finding things in those numbers that no one up until him had a clue could possibly be there. I was hooked, and I have been addicted ever since. In fact, Bill James changed the entire trajectory of my life.

I began working with Bill James a few years after that and wound up changing my career to focus full time on baseball analysis. As much as I loved tinkering with the numbers of insurance, working with the numbers of baseball was a dream come true.

◆ ◆ ◆

Now, I don't expect many people to be as nuts as I am about numbers and statistics. And I certainly don't expect anyone to quit his or her job to become a baseball statistical analyst. That is why I was so pleasantly surprised to read this book by Glenn Guzzo. Here was an explanation of baseball statistics not for people like me or Bill James, but for the "casual fan"—people just getting into baseball stats, veteran statheads trying to explain to their significant others why they care about stats, and as a gift for kids just becoming interested in baseball statistics.

Here you will learn why batting average isn't the only—or even the best—way to judge a hitter. You will learn about the nuances of reading a boxscore—how you can see the story of the game from its hidden secrets. You will learn as much as you need—or want—to know about why and how statistics are kept and, more importantly, how knowing and understanding statistics can increase your enjoyment of the game.

You don't have to skip the hot dogs and beer. You can still admire the beautiful fields. You will still hold your breath on that collision at home. But if you read and digest this book, you will also understand many more of the moves that take place within a game, and why your team is in last place instead of first, and who should be chosen for the All-Star Game or the Hall of Fame…and who should not.

So, enjoy baseball any way you want. If the statistics of the game help, then by all means use them. If they don't, forget about it. Give your copy of *The New Ballgame* to someone else!

◆ ◆ ◆

But, just to show you how the revolution in baseball stats can help you enjoy baseball even more, I'll give you one last little example.

Remember that first baseball game that I went to with my dad? I wasn't sure exactly when the game was, or how old I was when I went, but I did have some very specific recollections about it. I knew it was a bat-day doubleheader, that the White Sox were playing the Los Angeles Angels, and that a player named Leon Wagner beat the Sox in extra innings with a triple.

Because of advances in technology, including the Internet and search engines, we have access to a lot more information today than we used to, and it is easier and cheaper and faster to find. Baseball statistics are part of that new world. There's a wonderful non-profit organization called Retrosheet that is recording the numbers of baseball by collecting old scoresheets and computerizing them. I went to their website (www.retrosheet.org) today, and within 10 minutes I found the exact date of my first baseball game, based on the little bit of information I had. It was May 12, 1963.

Amazing.

John Dewan

author of *The Fielding Bible*

TALKIN' BASEBALL

Statistics are the language of baseball.

That language is becoming harder to understand every year.

While watching a game on TV or enjoying a conversation about baseball, it seems to be getting as tough to rely on traditional statistics like batting average, earned run average, and runs batted in as it is to rely solely on English in Miami. We now have baseball's equivalent of Spanglish, with new terms such as OPS, WHIP and VORP mixed into sentences with runs, hits and errors.

If you need an interpreter, this book can help. This book is for you if:

- You have a recently-acquired affection for baseball and need a guilt-free way to get up to speed.
- You have a recently-acquired affection for a baseball *fan* and want to understand just what in the world he or she is talking about.

- You have always liked baseball, but have fallen behind on the new numbers discussed so casually on TV and in the office fantasy baseball leagues.
- Every time you go to a ballgame as a social event you feel like an outsider, unable to decipher the insider talk around you.
- You are curious about simulation games like Rotisserie (fantasy) baseball or Strat-O-Matic.

The good news: Most of this stats talk is pretty simple (although if you *like* advanced mathematics you can put that to use too) and help is everywhere—in this book, on the Internet, and possibly even in the seat next to you at the ballpark.

The bad news: There is no way around all this "stats stuff" if you want to be even moderately literate in baseball.

Sure, you can go to a stadium and savor the sights, sounds, smells and tastes of the game. Hot dogs sizzling on the grill, freshly mowed outfield grass greener than you can ever make your own lawn, thrilled crowds roaring as one voice against a backdrop of red-white-and-blue—all of the Americana is still there.

But the handwriting—and the numbers—is on the wall if the person you go to a game with has only thirty seconds for your chatter about how the kids love that mascot, but three innings for non-stop repartee with a stranger about game strategy, baseball trivia, and whether any team with Alex Rodriguez will ever win a World Series.

True, the beauty of the game and the majesty of its heroes have inspired poetry, song, film and theater. But listen to any conversation with baseball fans and you'll hear much less rhapsody about green cathedrals, setting suns, and the smack of horsehide against oiled leather than raves about the statistical pace Albert Pujols has set in his awesome first six years, or rants about whether Barry Bonds will hit more home runs than Hank Aaron.

◆ ◆ ◆

Baseball is more statistically-minded than any other sport, and that accounts for its memorable history. Thanks to their statistical achievements, yesteryear's players are remembered—and revered—by fans who never saw them. Numeric milestones achieved generations ago have contemporary value as old records are approached and new ones set. It is impossible to discuss Barry Bonds' power hitting today without also bringing up Hank Aaron, who played from the 1950s to the 1970s, and Babe Ruth, who played from the 1910s to the 1930s. Few devoted football fans can cite the record for most career passing yards or rushing yards, but few devoted baseball fans would not be able to identify Aaron by the number 755 and Ruth by 714—their career totals for home runs.

Better than the name and number on his jersey, a player's statistics tell him apart from other players. His statistics define him: Describe one player as a .300 hitter and you honor him; label him a .250 hitter and you impugn him, even though the difference is but one hit per week. A 20-game winner is the designer brand among pitchers; a 10-game winner is generic.

Each generation has deepened baseball's relationship with its statistics. This is not further evidence that the apocalypse is near, but natural evolution. Statistics gain meaning with time—when Nap Lajoie hit .422 in the first year of "modern" baseball (1901), no one knew how special that was. When

Rogers Hornsby topped that by hitting .424 in 1924, who knew that only two more men would ever hit even .400? Or that in 2007 we would reach the 66th anniversary of the last man to do it? (Ted Williams hit .406 in 1941.) With more history behind us, hindsight makes context and significance clearer. Better technology reveals more information and gives us more tools with which to understand history.

Look at the plaques on display in the National Baseball Hall of Fame and Museum in Cooperstown, New York, for two of the game's greatest players, Ty Cobb and Willie Mays.

TYRUS RAYMOND COBB
Detroit-Philadelphia, AL—1906-1928

Led American League in batting twelve times and created or equaled more Major League records than any other player. Retired with 4,191 Major League hits.

WILLIE HOWARD MAYS, JR.
"The Say Hey Kid"
New York, NL, San Francisco, NL, New York, NL, 1951-1973

One of baseball's most colorful and exciting stars. Excelled in all phases of the game. Third in homers (660), runs (1,062) and total bases (6,066); seventh in hits (3,283) and RBI's (1,903). First in putouts by outfielder (7,095). First to top both 300 homers and 300 steals. Led league in batting once, slugging five times, home runs and steals four seasons. Voted NL MVP in 1954 and 1965. Played in 24 All-Star games—a record.

Both men were superstar outfielders, excelling at bat, on the bases, and in the field. Both led their teams to several World Series. Both were considered the best players of their day—and, for many fans, the greatest players ever. Both were elected to the Hall of Fame as soon as they were eligible, with more votes than any other players being considered with them. So what is the difference between Cobb's terse tribute—despite setting "more Major League records than any other player"—and the detailed accounting of Mays' magnificence? Cobb's plaque was crafted after he was elected with the first Hall of Fame class in 1936. Mays' plaque was written in 1979.

In 1936, the most devoted adult baseball fans had seen Cobb and almost every player in modern baseball. Since 1901 the major leagues were confined to ten host cities no further west than St. Louis. The Hall of Fame electorate knew Cobb was in an elite class because they had seen it with their own eyes. His statistics were important, but secondary to what the voters knew about Cobb's place in the history of the game.

By 1979, the men Mays was compared to were legends—known by oral histories, written baseball "scripture," and grainy frames of film. Anyone fifty years old in 1979 would not yet have been born when Cobb played his last season, and would not have witnessed the play of other superstar outfielders, such as Tris Speaker, Joe Jackson, Ed Delahanty, Sam Crawford, Babe Ruth and others. Most of all, these greats of the game were known in 1979 by their major league statistics. To establish Mays' rightful place alongside them in the Hall of Fame, his numbers had to stand up to theirs. That was the most ready means of comparison.

With time, baseball has grown ever more dependent on its numbers. It has now reached the point where it is nearly impossible to watch a game without a player's worth being measured by his statistics—those of the current season and game, but also the trend over recent seasons and his career. Statistics dominate ballpark scoreboards and the graphics that flash every inning of every televised game. Trivia questions, typically based on statistics, accompany almost every game.

◆ ◆ ◆

Statistics widen baseball's popularity. ESPN's *SportsCenter* and *Baseball Tonight* spend about as much time on statistics as they do on filmed highlights. A growing number of fans (currently estimated at four million) spend time each day in statistics-driven fantasy baseball leagues than frequently attend games. Preseason magazines devoted to fantasy baseball now outnumber traditional spring annuals. Those publishers bold enough to offer a "pure" preseason magazine (*The Sporting News*, among the very few) offer a separate magazine exclusively targeting fantasy baseball players, while still loading their traditional publication with stats. Statistics are the engines for computer game and board game simulations like Strat-O-Matic. Competing for bragging rights or money, fantasy leaguers and simulation gamers scout for the next superstars and gain insight about more ballplayers than they ever would without their games. With the major leagues now in nearly three times as many cities than in Ty Cobb's day, a fan who knows the talent on every team is almost certainly a fantasy or simulation player.

It's fair to say that statistics have even saved baseball from its self-destructive labor problems. When a late-season 1994 players strike had the ultimate consequence—the World Series was canceled for the first time—bitter fans turned their backs on the game. Major League Baseball didn't fully recover until 1998, when Cardinals slugger Mark McGwire and Cubs power hitter Sammy Sosa threatened, then overtook, the single-season home run record that had gone unchallenged for thirty-seven years. McGwire and Sosa's thrilling home run derby invoked fans' memories of the great Yankee slugging duos—Roger Maris and Mickey Mantle, Babe Ruth and Lou Gehrig. Fans turned out in huge numbers hoping to see the statistical record fall. When McGwire was the first to break Roger Maris' record of 61 home runs, he earned a prominent place on Page One of hundreds of daily newspapers, including *The New York Times*, where sports rarely earn front-page status. For the record, McGwire ended that season with 70 homers; Sosa had 66.

The statistics pay off, too. Players who produce big numbers get big paychecks. Teams competing for wins and economic prosperity employ full-time analysts to determine which statistics are worth investing in. More than ever, big-league general managers are younger and more statistically savvy. Michael Lewis' 2003 book *Moneyball*, devoted to all of these trends, became a bestseller and a household (well, a front office/locker room/dugout) name.

If this expanding landscape looks like a daunting adventure, we offer some encouragement. *The New Ballgame* is organized to help you digest as much or as little as you want and at your own pace. Use it to expand your comfort zone at the ballpark, in front of your TV, or in office chatter. While you might not be able to outdo the greatest baseball statistical minds like Bill James, Rob Neyer or John Dewan, you will be able to hold your own in a conversation about the numbers of baseball.

This way, the next time someone takes you out to the ballpark, you'll be able to truly appreciate the new ballgame.

EVERYDAY STATISTICS

These terms are used in casual conversation among typical baseball fans. Most of these terms will be used elsewhere in this book, so it's time to make sure our language is understood.

NOTE: There are rare exceptions to some of the definitions described here.

BATTING

At-Bats (AB)

Every time a player gets into the batter's box, he is at bat. But he doesn't get credit for an official *at-bat* unless he gets a hit, makes an out, or reaches base on an error (which should have been an out if the fielder had handled the play effectively). When a player reaches base on a fielder's choice (which usually results in a teammate being out) that also counts as an at-bat.

Plate Appearance (PA)

All official at-bats are plate appearances. So are the other results that don't count as an official at-bat—mostly this happens when the batter walks, gets hit by a pitch, makes a successful sacrifice bunt, or hits a sacrifice fly.

Batting Average (BA or AVG)

This is the most common expression of a player's hitting ability. It is computed by dividing the player's hits (singles, doubles, triples, and home runs) by his at-bats (Hits/AB). This statistic is expressed as a three-digit decimal, such as .265 or .300.

A mediocre average in most seasons is .260 to .270. A .300 average—just 3 hits for every 10 at-bats—is often enough to rank a player among the top 20 batting averages in his league. A batting average of .330 to .360 is usually necessary to win the league batting title. The last time any player hit .400 or more in one season was in 1941, when Ted Williams hit .406 for the Boston Red Sox in the American League. The last National League player to hit .400 was Bill Terry, who hit .401 in 1930.

Batting average, however, measures only hits, not all the times a player helps his team by getting on base, nor how far the batter advances on his hits. Because of this, batting average is slowly, but steadily, giving way to its cousins—on base-average and slugging percentage.

On-Base Average (OBA) or On-Base Percentage (OBP)

Divide the total number of hits, all bases on balls, and hit by pitch by the total number of at-bats, all bases on balls, hit by pitch, and sacrifice flies. This will yield a number that is expressed like batting average, only it's higher: In a year when the league batting average is .265, the OBP might be .335.

Individually, an on-base percentage of .400 is very good, but not rare. An on-base percentage of .500 is supreme—the combination of a high batting average and an extraordinary number of walks. Babe Ruth eclipsed .500 five times. Ted Williams did it three times. Barry Bonds did it every year from 2001 to 2004. And in 2004, when Bonds was walked intentionally an unheard-of 120 times, for an equally unheard-of grand total of 232 walks, his on-base percentage was a record .609.

On-base percentage is perhaps used most in conjunction with—or in contrast to—batting average. For example, a speedy .270-hitting shortstop who seldom walks may have an on-base percentage of barely more than .300. His manager may be tempted to use him as a leadoff hitter, but with an on-base percentage far below the league norm, he isn't on base often enough to take full advantage of that speed, or to set up enough run-scoring hits for the powerful hitters behind him.

Aggressiveness at the plate has its virtue, but players with low on-base averages make a lot of outs. Typically, they do so in the worst way—swinging at pitches out of the strike zone. In turn, they get fewer good pitches to hit, because opposing pitchers know that such a batter is not going to be selective enough to demand one.

Total Bases (TB)

This is the sum of all bases achieved by a batter on his hits—and only his hits. Singles count as one total base, doubles two, triples three, and home runs four. We need this statistic to compute slugging percentage.

Slugging Percentage (SLG)

Total bases divided by at-bats (TB / AB). This statistic is expressed as a three-digit decimal (e.g. .450), just like BA and OBP. Slugging percentage describes a hitter's power. An impressive full-season slugging percentage is .500 or higher. A slugging percentage of .600 or more is exceptional. Once in a while a batter will reach a .700 slugging percentage. This feat happens roughly every three years and is achieved by the most legendary sluggers: Lou Gehrig, Ted Williams, Mickey Mantle, Mark McGwire, and a dozen others. Only Babe Ruth and Barry Bonds have had single-season slugging percentages higher than .800.

On-Base Plus Slugging (OPS)

This is steadily becoming the coin of the realm to determine a player's value as a hitter. It adds on-base percentage and slugging percentage to produce a new number expressed with a decimal.

First basemen and slugging corner outfielders often reach a .900 OPS (with a .360 OBP and a .540 SLG, for instance). An .800 OPS is a solid mark for a catcher or middle infielder.

It is possible to exceed a 1.000 ("one thousand") OPS. Barry Bonds, Todd Helton, Manny Ramirez and Frank Thomas have done so repeatedly. Therefore, OPS also can be expressed without the decimal – as 1025, for instance, or 921, or 776.

The most serious statistics analysts multiply OPS by slugging, rather than adding them. But the much simpler addition produces a number accurate enough for most stat-minded fans.

Runs (R) and Runs Batted In (RBI)

The player who crosses home plate before the third out of an inning scores a run. The player whose batted ball causes the run to score gets credit for a run batted in. The batter does not get credit for an RBI if his batted ball results in an error that causes the run to score, nor if the batter hits into a double play. A batter can get credit for a run batted in without swinging the bat at all—if he walks or is hit by a pitch when the bases were loaded, which forces the man on third to home with a run. No run batted in is credited if the run scores on a wild pitch, passed ball, or balk.

Single-season milestones are 100 for runs scored and 100 for runs batted in.

Sacrifice (SH)

A batter who bunts with the intention of making an out so that his teammate on base can advance gets credit for a sacrifice, and is not charged a time at bat. If, however, the bunter is not effective—the defense retires the teammate baserunner after all—the bunter does not get credit for a sacrifice and is charged with a time at bat. A batter who takes a full swing and is put out does not get credit for a sacrifice, even if his teammate(s) on base advance.

Sacrifice Fly (SF)

A flyball that is caught for the first or second out of an inning (or should have been, but was dropped for an error), yet scores a baserunner, is a sacrifice fly. The batter gets credit for a run batted in and is not charged a time at-bat.

Stolen Base (SB)

A baserunner is credited with a stolen base only when he advances on his own speed without a teammate hitting the ball or otherwise getting on base. No stolen base is credited to the baserunner who advances on a wild pitch, passed ball, or balk. Nor is a stolen base credited if the defense is indifferent to the runner's advance. This last situation usually happens late in games when the team on defense is ahead by more than one run. Then, it may decide not to keep the runner close to his base, nor throw to get him out. That is called "defensive indifference."

Caught Stealing (CS)

Obviously, if a player is thrown out attempting to steal, he is caught stealing. Less obviously, if he is picked off by a pitcher or catcher's throw without attempting to advance to the next base, this does *not* count as a caught stealing.

PITCHING

Win (W)

A pitcher gets a win either when he pitches the entire game of a victory or is replaced when his team has a lead that it never relinquishes.

For example, if Randy Johnson leaves with his New York Yankees leading 5-2 and the Yankees win 5-4, Johnson is the winning pitcher. If he leaves with a 5-2 lead, but the Red Sox come back to tie it and then the Yankees finally prevail after all, Johnson is *not* the winning pitcher. A teammate who was the pitcher when the Yankees went ahead for good will get that win.

A pitcher whose team was tied or trailing when he was pinch hit for can get the win if his team goes ahead while at-bat in the same inning as the pinch hit—provided, of course, that the team never loses that lead.

To win, a starting pitcher must pitch at least five innings. There are cases where a reliever has won without even throwing a pitch! (By recording an out by picking off a runner, for instance, and then his team goes ahead in their next turn at bat.)

Loss (L)

The rules governing a loss are similar to those for a win. The losing pitcher is the pitcher who is charged with the run that puts his team behind for good.

A pitcher is responsible for any runners he leaves on base. Therefore, a pitcher who leaves the game with a lead can still be charged with the loss if he departs after allowing the potential lead run to reach base and that man comes around to score while another pitcher is on the mound. Those runs are charged to the pitcher who put them on base, not to the relief pitcher who allowed the hits that scored those inherited runners.

A pitcher who departs when his team is trailing can be spared a loss if, at any subsequent point in the game, his team comes back to tie or take the lead. If his team does this, but eventually loses anyway, the loss is charged to the teammate who surrendered the run that put his team behind for good.

A starting pitcher does not have to pitch five innings to get a loss. There are numerous cases where the losing pitcher started the game and failed to get out a single batter before giving up the eventual winning run.

Save (S or SV)

The official MLB rule book describes this somewhat complicated system as well as anything:

> Credit a pitcher with a save when he meets all three of the following conditions: (1) He is the finishing pitcher in a game won by his club; and (2) He is not the winning pitcher; and (3) He qualifies under one of the following conditions:
>
> (a) He enters the game with a lead of no more than three runs and pitches for at least one inning; or
>
> (b) He enters the game, regardless of the count, with the potential tying run either on base, or at-bat, or on deck (that is, the potential tying run is either already on base or is one of the first two batsmen he faces); or
>
> (c) He pitches effectively for at least three innings. No more than one save may be credited in each game.

Therefore, only relief pitchers earn saves. The relief pitchers who do so are called "closers."

Earned Run Average (ERA)

This is the number of earned runs (ER)—runs that are charged against the pitcher rather than to defensive mistakes—per nine innings pitched.

To compute ERA, multiply the number of earned runs allowed by 9, then divide by innings pitched.

Runs attributable to fielding errors, passed balls, and some other rare plays are *unearned runs* and do not count in the calculation of earned run average.

Innings Pitched (IP)

The number of innings a pitcher completed, expressed as units of three outs each. For instance, a relief pitcher who gets one out before being replaced has pitched one-third of an inning. If, the next time he pitches, he gets two outs before being replaced, he has pitched an additional two-thirds of an inning and his total for the two outings is one inning (not two).

For convenience in small-print box scores and in spreadsheets, partial innings are often written with decimal points. One-third of an inning is 0.1 innings; two-thirds is 0.2 innings. Because this can be confusing outside of box scores, a pitcher's total innings are often rounded off to the closest whole inning—rounded down if the pitcher has pitched an extra one-third of an inning and rounded up if he has pitched an extra two-thirds of an inning.

Complete Game (CG)

This is counted only when the starting pitcher can pitch a complete game. However, he doesn't necessarily have to pitch nine innings to get credit for a complete game.

A losing pitcher who pitches eight innings against a home team that does not need to bat in the bottom of the ninth inning gets a complete game. So does a pitcher who has pitched all of the innings in a shortened, but legally complete game (usually, one that has gone at least five innings before weather, curfew or another problem ends the game).

> *NOTE: A relief pitcher who is his team's final pitcher in that game gets credit for a Game Finished (GF). This is strictly a relief pitcher's stat. A starting pitcher who pitches a complete game does not and cannot get a GF.*

Shutout (SHO)

When a starting pitcher completes a game and allows no runs, he has pitched a shutout. If he has allowed any runs—even if they are all unearned runs—it cannot be a shutout. If he allows no runs, but doesn't complete the game, he does not get credit for a shutout.

FIELDING

Error (E)

Any time a batter reaches base or a runner takes an extra base because a fielder dropped a ball or made a bad throw, it is an error. Errors can occur without a ball being hit—a catcher might overthrow second base when a runner tries to steal; a pitcher might make an errant throw trying to pick a runner off base. It's also an error if a fielder drops a popup or flyball in foul territory, allowing the batter to get another chance instead of being out.

Not all fielding misplays are errors, however.

Wild pitches and passed balls (see below) are not errors.

If a line drive or groundball is hit so wickedly that all the fielder can do is slow it down, the official scorer is likely to score that a hit, not an error.

If a player misjudges a popup or flyball and it hits the ground without any fielder touching it, that usually will be scored a hit, not an error. However, a groundball that goes through a fielder's legs untouched almost always will be scored an error.

The rules also specify that official scorers are not permitted to anticipate a double play. Let's say the shortstop makes a perfect throw to second base to get a force out, then the second baseman pivots and throws wide of first, pulling the first baseman off the bag and allowing the batter to be safe. Although a good throw would have put the runner out, this will not be scored an error. However, if the second baseman's throw was so bad that the batter also made it to second, an error would be charged to the second baseman because the batter got an extra base.

Putout (PO)

The player who catches the ball or tags the runner for the out gets credit for a putout. First basemen get putouts on throws by infielders after groundballs. Catchers get putouts on strikeouts.

Assist (A or Ast)

The player(s) who throws or directs the ball to the fielder making the putout gets an assist. An infielder gets an assist after fielding a groundball and throwing it to the first baseman in time for the out. A pitcher gets an assist if a ball is hit off his body, then is fielded by a teammate and thrown for a putout. More than one assist is possible on a play. One example is a cutoff play involving two throws—one by the outfielder, then one by an infielder for a runner thrown out on the bases. A rundown that involves several throws before the putout is another.

Fielder's Choice (FC)

When the batter reaches base, but a teammate is put out because the fielders chose to make a play on the runner, the batter has hit into a fielder's choice. This counts the same as an out for computing his batting average—one time at-bat, no hit. On certain plays requiring a tag, even if the baserunner and the batter are both safe, it counts as a fielder's choice.

Double Play (DP) and Grounded Into Double Play (GIDP or GDP)

When the team in the field records two outs on a single time at-bat, it is a double play. This can happen many ways: a catch followed by throwing out a runner; a strikeout followed by throwing out a base stealer; a line drive caught by an infielder who then steps on the base before the runner can return, etc.

Most of these are considered baserunning mistakes. When a double play happens on a groundball, it is a GIDP. This statistic is kept separately for batters as an indication of the double plays that were the batter's fault.

A few very fast runners, usually left-handed hitters who bat leadoff and thus seldom bat with other runners on first base, hit into few, if any, groundball double plays for a season. Hard-hitting, right-handed sluggers with little speed, who bat in the middle of the lineup and therefore often bat with runners on first base, might hit into 20-25 double plays in a season.

Fielding Percentage (Fpct or Favg)

This is the percentage of successful plays by a fielder, normally expressed as a three-digit decimal. Add his putouts and assists, then divide that sum by his number of fielding chances (putouts plus assists plus errors). A fielder with no errors and at least one putout or assist is fielding 1.000 (expressed as "one thousand").

Wild Pitch (WP)

A pitch to home plate deemed *uncatchable* that escapes the catcher and permits one or more runners to advance a base is a wild pitch. If no runner advances, there is no wild pitch, no matter how errant the toss.

Passed Ball (PB)

A pitch to home plate deemed *catchable* but that escapes the catcher anyway and permits one or more runners to advance a base is a passed ball. If no runner advances, there is no passed ball, no matter how far the ball traveled.

Balk (BK)

When a runner is on base, once a pitcher has begun his movement towards home plate for a pitch, he must complete that throw in a continuous motion. If he hesitates, stops, changes direction, or does anything to disrupt that motion (e.g. accidentally drops the ball), he has committed a balk. The penalty for a balk is that all runners move up one base. Balks are most often committed by pitchers who try to deceive the baserunner(s). This can be done several ways, but often by throwing to the base after making a motion towards home.

SPECIAL EVENTS
No-Hitter

This happens when a starting pitcher completes a game allowing no hits. Walks, hit batsmen, errors, and other events that allow runners to reach base do not spoil a no-hitter. Only singles, doubles, triples and home runs do. A pitcher can allow a run (or more)—and even lose the game—despite pitching a no-hitter. It has happened several times.

Perfect Game

A starting pitcher has thrown a perfect game when he completes a game allowing no baserunners at all—even a runner who reaches base on a fielding error spoils a perfect game.

Cycle

A player has hit for the cycle when he gets a single, double, triple and home run in the same game.

Official major league rules can be found online at:
http://mlb.mlb.com/NASApp/mlb/mlb/official_info/official_rules/foreword.jsp

WHY BASEBALL ARGUMENTS NEVER END

A Brief Statistical History of Baseball

Baseball is the ultimate second-guessing game. There's enough time between pitches to think about the possibilities. There's enough time between batters to think about the alternatives. There are enough strategic moves in a typical game to think about what could have been. Fans who have "owned" their own salaried players in fantasy baseball leagues and who have "managed" 1,000 or more games with simulations like Strat-O-

Matic are *sure* they know better. They've been there, done that, enjoyed the same successes and wallowed in the same mistakes as the real managers and GMs. Second-guessed daily, exasperated big-league managers lament that their decisions are brilliant when they work and dumb when they don't.

A competitive sport played by competitive people and enjoyed by competitive fans, baseball is fertile for passionate argument and scholarly analysis. But it's tough to win those debates about what we've learned from the past and what we can expect in the future, or which teams and which players are the best (now, and all-time). For all of the new data (statistics) we acquire and the ever-improving means to analyze it, the *art* of baseball—performance on the field—stays ahead of the science. Just when we think that 100-plus years of study means we've seen enough baseball, or at least enough of the game's box scores, to be immune to surprise, along comes a team like the 2005 Chicago White Sox—who not only out-performed expectations, but even out-performed (in wins) all the statistics they produced. Baseball keeps surprising us. It's a team game, after all, and team-dependent statistics are serpentine, making cause and effect difficult to isolate. For every general statement one alert fan wants to make about the game and its players, another alert fan is going to be able to cite the noteworthy exceptions that disprove the absolute truth of the first claim.

This chapter is designed to help you become a more alert fan.

So remember:

It's a team game

- Teams underachieve when star players under-perform. They over-achieve when enough lesser players have career years. Before the

2005 season, almost nobody picked the Chicago White Sox to win it all. Even rarer was the forecaster (general manager, media analyst, or fantasy-league expert)—if there was one—who predicted that White Sox pitcher Jon Garland would finally fulfill his potential, winning 18 games, losing 10, and producing a fine 3.39 ERA. In five previous years with the Sox, Garland had a combined won-lost record of 46-51, a career ERA of 4.68 (never better than 4.38), and had never won more than 12 games in a season. A team without a dominant superstar, the Sox enjoyed career seasons from Garland, Jose Contreras, Neal Cotts, Cliff Politte, and catcher A.J. Pierzynski, who hit 18 home runs after never hitting more than 11 in any other season. The Sox got dramatic rebound seasons from outfielders Jermaine Dye and Scott Podsednik, third baseman Joe Crede, designated hitter Carl Everett, and pitchers Freddy Garcia and Mark Buehrle, whose performances all had been in decline for one or more years. The Sox depended heavily on the unexpectedly strong rookie contributions of second baseman Tadahito Iguchi and pitcher Bobby Jenks.

No doubt, the improvement by some of these players fueled the improvement by others. Starting pitchers, for instance, win more and pitch more innings if their teammates hit better. They have lower ERAs if the relief pitchers who succeed them are more brilliant than ever.

Give much credit for the Sox success to Chicago General Manager Ken Williams and Manager Ozzie Guillen for assembling the parts and getting the whole to exceed the sum (if the Sox had won only as many games as their runs scored-runs allowed differential said they should win, they would not even have made it into the postseason). But few people are optimistic enough to project so much simultaneous improvement by so many players.

Moving parts

- Trades and free-agency keep changing individual and team fortunes. Despite their first World Series victory since 1917, the Sox made significant changes after sharing the champagne bottles. Almost every Chicago player who did not improve in 2005—outfielder Aaron Rowand, designated hitter Frank Thomas, and pitchers Orlando Hernandez and Damaso Marte—started 2006 on another team. They were replaced principally by designated hitter Jim Thome and pitcher Javier Vazquez—who both underperformed for other teams in 2005—and rookie outfielder Brian Anderson.

  Different surroundings—a new supporting cast of teammates, a new ballpark, maybe a switch between the American and National leagues that presents new opponents—can have dramatic effects on player performance, for better or for worse.

The "law of averages"

- Better described as random variation or better still as Insufficient Sample (the two most important words in statistics), the classic illustration of Insufficient Sample is probably apocryphal, but here goes: The chancellor at the University of North Carolina wanted to know which degree majors produced the highest salaries in the real world. The study he commissioned returned this startling discovery: geography. It turns out there were only three graduates with geography majors, and one of them was Michael Jordan.

This is not the book to discuss standard deviation, regression to the mean, and other sophisticated math (you can thank my editor for keeping me in line), but know this: Much of what happens in a mere 500 at-bats or 200 innings pitched is subject to chance.

Most of Podsednik's batting decline between 2003 and 2004 and his rebound in 2005 (from a .314 batting average in 2003 to .249 and back to .290) can be explained by normal statistical fluctuations in the life of a player his age. It sounds like denial, but when a player dismisses a batting slump by saying that his line drives "are just not falling in this year," it's probably true. That's not very satisfying. We'd rather understand that this guy has messed up his swing or that he's really not very good. But recent studies show that balls in play behave pretty much the same for everyone. The players who hit better put more balls in play (fewer strikeouts) and/or hit more fair balls out of play (home runs). Pitchers who perform better get more strikeouts, walk fewer batters, and keep the ball in the park. We told you this stuff is simple.

You won't find such stats in handy places, but players whose percentage of balls in play produced an abnormal amount of hits one year are good candidates for lower batting averages the next, and vice versa. Similarly, teams that win an extraordinarily high number of one-run games one year are likeliest to decline in the standings next season.

The White Sox' 35-19 record in one-run games in 2005—by far the best in the major leagues—foretold their decline in 2006. The Sox' performance in one-run games dropped to 24-21 and their win total dropped from 99 in 2005 to 90 in 2006.

Yes, good teams get most of the good luck. "Luck," as famed former general manager Branch Rickey famously said, "is the residue of design." But abnormal good luck is one of the toughest things to reproduce. If that wasn't true, we wouldn't have had seven different teams win the last seven World Series.

THE SHORT SERIES

Nothing in baseball illustrates Insufficient Sample better than the postseason. These best-of-seven-game series are not microcosms of the 162-game regular season. They are abbreviated competitions that often turn on a single game, or even a single play. The margin can be razor thin—so thin, that on several unforgettable occasions, the defining moment has been determined not by a clutch hit or a player's gaffe, but by an umpire's call or a fan's interference with a catchable ball. If you have any skepticism about this, just see how long it takes any fan of the St. Louis Cardinals or Kansas City Royals to recognize the name of Don Denkinger, any fan of the Chicago Cubs or Florida Marlins to recognize the name of Steve Bartman, any fan of the New York Yankees or Baltimore Orioles to recognize the name of Jeffrey Maier. You will not, however, find these names on your stat sheets.

Major League Baseball began allowing second-place teams (Wild Card teams) into the postseason in 1995 as part of its recovery plan from the destructive 1994 players' strike and canceled World Series. In the first twelve seasons under that system, the team with the best record in baseball for the regular season made it to the World Series just five times and won it only once (and not since 1998). Only twice have the teams with the best American League and National League records faced each other in the World Series (and not since 1999).

In contrast, Wild Card teams have reached the World Series seven times (five straight from 2002 to 2006) and won four, including each year from 2002 (when both World Series teams, Anaheim and San Francisco, were Wild Card teams) through 2004.

Some see injustice in this. They speak of the integrity of the 162-game schedule and tradition. From the first World Series in 1903 through 1968, only the most successful team from each league qualified for the postseason. From 1969 to 1993, World Series teams first had to be division winners (only two divisions per league then). These traditionalists are outraged that today, teams not good enough to even win one of three divisions in their league can win the ultimate prize just by going on a hot streak.

Others see poetic justice in this. The New York Yankees, who buy new stars annually with a payroll twice, even five times, greater than other teams, have won their division almost every year (ten of twelve and every season since 1998), but have not won a World Series since 2000. Those who are happy about this speak of the integrity of the seven-game series—that you can't buy a World Series, at least not with a money-back guarantee.

The grid on the following page shows how the World Series actually played out over the last twelve years versus how it would have been under the old rules.

WILD WORLD SERIES

Teams in **Bold** had the best record in baseball that season
Teams in *Italic* were Wild Card teams

Year	WS Winner	WS Loser	Best Records: AL–NL
2006	St. Louis	*Detroit*	**NY Yankees–NY Mets**
2005	Chicago WS	*Houston*	Chicago WS–**St. Louis**
2004	*Boston*	**St. Louis**	NY Yankees–**St. Louis**
2003	*Florida*	**NY Yankees**	**NY Yankees–Atlanta**
2002	*Anaheim*	*San Francisco*	**NY Yankees/Oakland**–Atlanta
2001	Arizona	NY Yankees	**Seattle**–Houston
2000	NY Yankees	*NY Mets*	Chicago WS–**San Francisco**
1999	NY Yankees	**Atlanta**	NY Yankees–**Atlanta**
1998	**NY Yankees**	San Diego	**NY Yankees**–Atlanta
1997	*Florida*	Cleveland	Baltimore–**Atlanta**
1996	NY Yankees	Atlanta	**Cleveland**–Atlanta
1995	Atlanta	**Cleveland**	**Cleveland**–Atlanta

Eleven different franchises have played for the World Series in the past seven years. Only the Yankees and Cardinals have played in more than one of those. Every one of those Series would have had a different match-up if only the teams with the best record in each league had advanced to the Fall Classic.

Say this for MLB's Wild Card system—the Wild Card is always a good team. In contrast, by letting more than half of their teams into the playoffs, the National Basketball Association and National Hockey League create faux drama for sub-.500 teams struggling to reach the postseason, where they are promptly eliminated in front of fans who paid double the regular season ticket prices.

THE LONG AND WINDING ROAD

Fans get pumped up over the game's great rivalries (Yankees-Red Sox, Dodgers-Giants, Cubs-Cardinals). They argue passionately about who is the best player (Albert Pujols? Alex Rodriguez? Barry Bonds? Derek Jeter?). But the debates that always go extra innings are the ones about the players and teams who are the best ever. The fascinating fuss over whether Bonds used steroids is exponentially louder because he has achieved home run records that elevate him to the ranks of Hank Aaron and Babe Ruth.

After death and taxes, the most inevitable fact of life is that baseball fans will argue the answers to questions like these: Who is the greatest left-handed pitcher? Who has been passed over for the Hall of Fame? Is Rafael Palmeiro really one of the greatest sluggers in the history of the game? Does Pedro Martinez belong in the same breath as Walter Johnson and Christy Mathewson?

These debates swirl like a hurricane because we want to compare players to those they never played against and to those we never saw.

For this elusive context we need proof, and statistics are the closest thing we have to scientific objectivity. But big-league baseball has evolved in many ways since the National League's formation in 1876, both confounding cross-era comparisons and making them more fun to argue. As revered statistical records fall and commentators make their cases for Hall of Fame candidacies and "best-ever" tags, keep in mind that competitive conditions vary by era, sometimes dramatically. Those changes in rules, ballparks, player usage, and other conditions can be used to make (or tear down) most any claim.

It's here that the famous quote from nineteenth century British Prime Minister Benjamin Disraeli gains traction in baseball: "There are lies, damn lies and statistics."

Dead Ball / Lively Ball

In the Dead Ball Era, prior to 1920, baseballs were mushier, easier for pitchers to doctor, and seldom removed from games. Darkened by tobacco juice, infield dirt, and general wear, the balls used in this era before lighted ballparks were tough to see by mid-game and even tougher to hit far.

Game tactics—and the statistics they produced—were radically different in the Dead Ball Era.

The leading home run hitters generally swatted seven to twelve in a season—just enough for a very good month today. Speed and defense were the essentials every manager looked for. Power was measured more by doubles and triples than home runs, and speed could get those extra bases. With little chance of hitting homers, batters bunted more and struck out less. Singles were responsible for more of the run-production, and players ran the bases with abandon. With little risk of losing home runs to innings shortened by baserunning outs, the comparative reward for an extra base was higher. Teams accepted the risk and were thrown out attempting to steal almost as often as they made it. For example, in 1911, the New York Giants won the National

League pennant by pitching well, hitting well, and setting a record with 347 stolen bases. Outfielder Fred Snodgrass, third in the league with 51 steals, was caught stealing 49 times. Outfielder Josh Devore, second in the league with 61 steals, was caught 41 times.

When Ty Cobb set a record with 96 stolen bases in 1915, he was the seventh man to steal 65 or more in a season between 1901 and 1919. Cobb himself did it five times. Once the Lively Ball era began in 1920, no one reached 65 stolen bases until 1962, when Cobb's record was finally overcome after 47 years.

In the Lively Ball Era, the ball was given a livelier cork center and more tightly stitched leather, resulting in many more home runs. As power gained prominence, stolen bases declined. Players who could clobber the livelier ball beyond the fences thirty times or more were now considered more valuable than men who could steal thirty bases, even if the sluggers' lack of speed cost their teams defensively. In 1920, big leaguers stole barely more than half the number of bases as

In 1930, the so-called "Year of the Hitter," the entire NL, pitchers included, hit .303. The Philadelphia Phillies hit .315—and finished last. They ended the season 40 games out of first place with the worst record in baseball (52-102), thanks to a worst-ever 6.71 team ERA.

The 1930 National League also featured the last NLer to hit .400 (Bill Terry, .401) and Hack Wilson, whose 191 RBIs that season have never been challenged and whose 56 home runs stood as the NL record until 1998.

IMPRESS YOUR FRIENDS • IMPRESS YOUR FRIENDS

Frank "Home Run" Baker never hit more than 12 home runs in a season, but won four consecutive American League home run titles for the Philadelphia Athletics from 1911 to 1914. He earned his nickname by hitting game-winning home runs in Games 2 and 3 of the 1911 World Series against the New York Giants' two future Hall of Fame pitchers—Rube Marquard and Christy Mathewson. Baker was elected to the Hall of Fame, too.

they had in the peak of Dead Ball Era daring. Steals dropped another 14% in 1921. By 1930, stolen bases were down by two-thirds from Dead Ball standards, and down by three-fourths in 1941, the last year before ballplayers began leaving by the dozens for World War II. In the 1950s, the entire major leagues were stealing 600-800 bases per year, down from 3,000-3,400 per season from 1909 to 1914. The entire American League stole only 250 bases in 1950, the low-water mark. Twenty-five *teams* stole more than that in Dead Ball seasons.

The Dead Ball conditions had corresponding effects on pitcher stats.

Lower power meant lower scores. League-wide earned run averages routinely were below 3.00 in the Dead Ball Era. They spiked immediately in 1920 and routinely were above 4.00 until the late 1950s. ERAs reached terrifying heights in the 1930 National League (4.97) and the 1936 American League (a record 5.04).

Since 1901, full-time pitchers have managed sterling 1.65 ERAs or better sixty-two times. Fifty-six of them were achieved in the Dead Ball Era.

More bunts, fewer strikeouts, and more outs on the bases meant fewer pitches to throw during the Dead Ball Era. Complete games were the norm—86% of all starts in 1901 and 58% by 1919. In 2005, that percentage was less than eight. The American League Central teams had the most complete games of any division in 2006—33. It took at least that many, usually more, for an *individual* pitcher to lead the American League in complete games every year from 1901 to 1917.

The talk of the 2005 postseason was how the Chicago White Sox played a throwback style, letting their starting pitchers throw deep into games. The 2005 Sox had the most stable starting-pitcher rotation in the American League. Their top four starters combined for 130 starts and 890 innings pitched, far above the twenty-first century norm. In 1906, the first time Chicago won a World Series, the top four White Sox pitchers started 121 times and threw 1,078 innings. That same year, 27 pitchers from the eight AL teams threw at least 210 innings, with five topping 300. In 2005, 10 pitchers from the 14 AL teams threw at least 210 innings, with the Sox' Mark Buehrle leading the way at 237.

Expansion / Integration

When it comes to baseball statistics, you can count on this: rabid debate over whether milestones achieved since 1961 are tainted by expansion.

Once the American League debuted in 1901, Major League Baseball had the same sixteen franchises (although some relocated) until its first expansion in 1961. Two teams were added to the American League then and two more to the National League in 1962. Four teams, two in each league, were added in 1969, the only time MLB has expanded by more than two teams in a season. Two more were added to the AL in 1977 and to the NL in 1993. Tampa Bay was added to the AL and Arizona to the NL in 1998, the latest expansion.

Offense typically spikes in the first two years after an expansion. Roger Maris hit his record 61 home runs in 1961. Mark McGwire and Sammy Sosa shattered Maris' mark in 1998. The explanation is simple and oft repeated: Expansion dilutes pitching talent so much that batters thrive. Of course, expansion adds lots of bad hitters, too. The truth is common sense—star players thrive when Triple-A level talent gets added to the big leagues. For instance, future Hall of Famers Reggie Jackson, Willie McCovey, Harmon Killebrew, Tom Seaver and Phil Niekro—plus Pete Rose—all had the best years of their careers in 1969, the year four teams were added to the major leagues. So did many other excellent veteran players.

However, expansion giveth and it taketh away. The addition of so many more teams and players has made some goals harder to achieve. From 1901 to 1967, baseball never went more than twelve years without a Triple Crown winner (that is, one player leading his league in batting average, home runs, and RBI). The thirteen winners in that interval include six winners in a sixteen-year period of the 1920s and 1930s (twice in four years by Rogers Hornsby). The great achievement occurred right on schedule when, in the first twenty-two seasons after World War II, four players did it (Boston's Ted Williams in 1947, New York's Mickey Mantle in 1956, Baltimore's Frank Robinson in 1966 and Boston's Carl Yastrzemski in 1967). But we are still waiting for the next one.

Fans of more recent players can retort that while the pre-World War II era may have been free of expansion, it also lacked the talent of black, Asian and most Latin players. Those original sixteen teams were built from a smaller population base and they refused to allow some of the best players to compete.

Ted Williams and Al Rosen each missed Triple Crowns by the narrowest margins. In 1949, Williams led the American League with 43 home runs and 159 RBI and officially hit .343, the same as batting champion George Kell of Detroit. But Kell won the crown—his .343 was .0002 higher than Williams. Williams would have been the only man to win the Triple Crown three times.

Four years later, Indians third baseman Al Rosen led the AL with 43 home runs and 145 runs batted in, but lost the Triple Crown by a half-step—he was thrown out by that much on his last at-bat of the season. Had he beaten the throw, Rosen, not Mickey Vernon, would have won the batting title. Rosen finished with a .336 average to Vernon's .337.

Even brighter than the dividing line between the sixteen-team major leagues and the expanded majors is the line between Dead Ball and Lively Ball eras. Perhaps nothing contributed more to extreme, record-setting performances than the condition of the ball. Most of the great pitching records belong to Dead Ball pitchers. The Hall of Fame is overrepresented by hitters from the 1920s and 1930s.

Integration and expansion complicate cross-era comparisons. That's why

In 1933, the Triple Crown was achieved in both the American League and National League, the only time this has ever happened. And it was done by two players from the same city! Philadelphia Athletics first baseman Jimmie Foxx hit .356 with 48 home runs and 163 runs batted in. Philadelphia Phillies outfielder Chuck Klein hit .368-28-120 (Klein's 28 home runs are the lowest of any Triple Crown winner in the Lively Ball era.)

the 1947 to 1960 period—post-integration, pre-expansion—is often called baseball's Golden Era. That period was rich in super-stars and historic moments:

- Jackie Robinson's debut (1947)
- Triple Crowns by Ted Williams (1947) and Mickey Mantle (1956)
- Three pennant races that finished in ties that had to be broken by dramatic play-offs (1948 AL, 1951 NL, 1959 NL)
- Bobby Thomson's playoff-winning home run for the Giants against the Dodgers (1951)
- Willie Mays' legendary over-the-shoulder catch on the titanic flyball hit by Vic Wertz in the World Series (1954)
- The only Brooklyn World Series victory (1955)
- The only perfect game in World Series history (1956)
- The only Milwaukee World Series victory (1957)

Although some of the greatest black and Latin superstars—Jackie Robinson, Mays, Hank Aaron, Frank Robinson, Ernie Banks, Lary Doby, Roberto Clemente and others—established themselves in this period, the Golden Era was not nearly as integrated as it could have been. The Detroit Tigers did not integrate until 1958 (Ozzie Virgil) and the Boston Red Sox were the last to integrate in 1959 (Pumpsie Green), both with part-time players. Because of its shallow reluctance to integrate, the American League missed out on much of the top talent. The AL's dismal All-Star Game record from 1951 to 1982 drives home the point: The AL lost 29 of 36 All-Star Games, reversing its previous dominance.

Spitters, Splitters and Sliders

The types of pitches batters have had to face in different eras has caused further inconsistencies in pitching and hitting statistics.

The spitball confounded hitters before WWII. At least five pitchers who relied on the spitball are in the Hall of Fame (Jack Chesbro, Ed Walsh, Stan Coveleski, Red Faber and Burleigh Grimes). Chesbro has the twentieth century record for wins in a season, 41, and Walsh once won 40. But the sloppy spitball was both unsanitary and dangerous because the tobacco-juiced lubricant darkened the ball in the time before lighted fields.

Ray Chapman didn't see one of those darkened baseballs in time. In the heat of a pennant race, the talented and popular Cleveland shortstop was hit in the head with a pitch from Carl Mays on August 17, 1920, and became the only player killed during a major league game. The *Washington Star* carried this remarkable account:

> *So terrific was the blow that the report of impact caused spectators to think the ball had struck his bat. Mays...acting under this impression, fielded the ball which rebounded halfway to the pitcher's box, and threw it to first base to retire Chapman.*

IMPRESS YOUR FRIENDS • IMPRESS YOUR FRIENDS •

A spitball figured in the most famous passed ball in history—the one that got away from Dodger catcher Mickey Owen in Game 4 of the 1941 World Series. The low pitch that struck out the Yankees' Tommy Henrich, with two outs in the ninth inning and Brooklyn leading, would have tied the Series at two games each. Instead, Henrich reached first after the ball eluded Owen and the Yankees went on to score four runs that inning, win the game and take a commanding 3-1 Series lead.

That was the only passed ball Owen committed all season. He has been remembered ever since for it. Almost forgotten was the pitcher, Hugh Casey. Years later, he admitted the pitch had been a spitball.

By most accounts, Mays was as nasty in disposition as his pitches. Although the pitch that killed Chapman was not believed to be a spitball (the submarine-style throwing Mays said it was a rising fastball), Chapman's death and the spitball's contribution to darkened baseballs accelerated the campaign to ban it. In 1921, only seventeen pitchers, whose livelihood depended on the pitch, were allowed to continue throwing it. Other pitchers have since been accused of throwing spitballs, and pitchers have continued to find other ways of doctoring baseballs to make sharper and less familiar movement. Officially, the last legal spitball was thrown in 1934, Burleigh Grimes' final season.

Chapman's death had another consequence: In 1921, umpires were instructed to replace balls more often. Having whiter, less lopsided balls to hit contributed to bigger offense in the Lively Ball era, too.

In the 1980s, pitchers like Bruce Sutter, Jack Morris and Mike Scott perfected the split-finger fastball, which imitated the spitball's sudden sinking action. That pitch got Sutter into the Hall of Fame, allowed Morris to become the winningest pitcher of the 1980s, and transformed Scott from a pedestrian pitcher to one of the most effective in the game.

In his first six seasons, Scott had a 29-44 win-loss record, gave up more hits than innings pitched, struck out fewer than four-and-a-half batters per nine innings, and had an ERA well above 4.00. In his next five seasons, Scott was 86-47, was one of baseball's least hittable pitchers, struck out about eight batters per nine innings, and had an ERA below 3.00. In 1986, Scott led the NL with a 2.22 ERA and 306 strikeouts.

Shortly after the spitball disappeared, along came the slider, another devastating and deceptive pitch that looks like a fastball but acts like a sharp curve, breaking late just as it crosses the plate. In *The Neyer/James Guide to Pitchers,* the authors date the slider roughly to 1936, but in their list of the "best sliders of all-time," all of the top ten pitchers began their careers after World War II. Among them are three Hall of Fame pitchers—Steve Carlton, Bob Gibson and Bob Lemon and a fourth, Randy Johnson, who will surely be inducted.

Hank Aaron, who knew something about hitting, predicted in the late 1960s that, because of the slider, there would never be another .400 hitter. He's been right for going on 40 years.

High Strike / Low Strike

As helpful as it is to know *who* threw the pitches and *what* pitches they threw, far more influential is *where* they were allowed to throw them. Nothing is a better predictor of swollen or shrunken hitting statistics than the strike zone's size and height. Periodic rule-tweaking has helped define baseball's different eras.

When the National League began play in 1876, the batter could demand high pitches (shoulders to waist), low pitches (waist to one foot above the ground) or "fair" ones (anywhere in between). But pitchers had all the other advantages: Walks counted as a time at-bat, but back then it took nine balls to earn one and the pitcher was only fifty feet away. Batters didn't get first base when hit by a pitch.

Batters could no longer dictate the strike zone beginning in 1887, and the strike zone definition—from the shoulders to the knees—was remarkably stable from 1887 through 1949. Changes in 1950, 1963 and 1969 influenced statistics dramatically.

When many of the game's brightest stars began going to war in 1941, offense started to decline. By 1945, more than 100 big-leaguers were in military service. The level of baseball talent was in disrepair, and so was the quality of the baseballs they hit. From 1942 to 1945, Spud Chandler (1.64), Hal Newhouser (1.81), Mort Cooper (1.77) and Howie Pollet (1.75) all won ERA titles with marks below 2.00—the norm in the Dead Ball era, but achieved only two other times since 1920. Even Joe DiMaggio, who had hit .381, .352 and .357 from 1939 to 1941, plummeted to a .305 average in 1942, at which point he began three years in the military. In 1986, DiMaggio told *Philadelphia Inquirer* sportswriter Frank Dolson that he enlisted, in part, because of what the poorly manufactured balls were doing to his batting average.

After the war, the arrival of outfielder Ralph Kiner in Pittsburgh and the development of New York Giants slugging first baseman Johnny Mize fueled a National League power surge, but otherwise offense was stagnant—until rule-makers shrank the strike zone in 1950. The new zone dropped from the shoulders to the armpits and from "the knees" to the top of the knees. The most difficult pitches to hit were now balls.

Batting averages immediately returned to pre-war levels and home runs shot up more than 17% in 1950. Home runs continued their ascent over the next decade, but otherwise pitchers reasserted their control—players swinging for the fences struck out more, batting averages settled into a .255-.265 norm, and run production was not dramatically different.

Until, that is, expansion arrived in 1961 and 1962. Roger Maris hit his 61 home runs and Warren Spahn's 3.01 ERA was good enough to top all NL pitchers in '61. Offense was even bigger in 1962, and Maury Wills broke Ty Cobb's enduring record by stealing 104 bases. In these two seasons, legitimate stars like Willie Mays, Frank Robinson, Hank Aaron and Mickey Mantle had huge seasons, but so did previously nondescript hitters like Norm Cash and Jim Gentile.

Two years of that was enough for the rule-makers, who in 1963 made the strike zone bigger than ever: "between the *top* of the batter's shoulders and his knees" (no longer *top* of the knees). That ushered in the best pitching era since Dead Ball times.

When most nostalgic fans talk about the period from 1963 to 1968, they remember superstar hitters like Mays, Aaron, Robinson, Roberto Clemente and Al Kaline. They recall promising rookies like Tony Oliva, Richie Allen and Tony Conigliaro. But the pitchers, not the hitters, were earning Hall of Fame credentials then.

Sandy Koufax, who began pitching well in 1961, was transcendent beginning in 1963 and each season until his premature retirement at his peak following the 1966 season. Juan Marichal and Bob Gibson were not far behind. Ferguson Jenkins, Gaylord Perry and Phil Niekro all had the good fortune to arrive during these years. So did such outstanding pitchers as Luis Tiant, Sam McDowell, Mickey Lolich and Mel Stottlemyre, though they fell short of Hall-of-Fame credentials.

The results of this change could not have been more dramatic. From 1962 to 1963, run scoring plummeted 11.6%, home runs dropped 10%, and batting averages declined sixteen points in the NL (to .245) and eight in the AL (to .247).

Then the hitting got really bad.

Some wonderful baseball history masked the numbers. Both leagues had legendary pennant races in 1964. Four AL teams were neck-and-neck in the last week of 1967. The Yankees' decline after two generations of dominance allowed the first AL pennants ever to fly over Minnesota and Baltimore. The 1964, 1965, 1967 and 1968 World Series all went the dramatic maximum seven games. Frank Robinson, freshly traded from Cincinnati to Baltimore, won the AL Triple Crown in 1966. Boston's Carl Yastrzemski duplicated the feat the next season. And there was the incomparable Koufax.

But these numbers don't lie: The already-depressed offensive numbers of 1966 took another huge plunge in 1967—the majors scored 700 fewer runs and hit 450 fewer homers, while the NL hit just .249 and the AL an embarrassing .236. Offense was now off 15.6% in runs and 23% in home runs since

1962. Already at bottom, offense took an incomprehensible new descent in 1968. The majors lost another 1,100 runs and more than 300 homers.

The 1968 season is now remembered as the Year of the Pitcher—the antithesis of 1930. Denny McLain won 31 games, baseball's first 30-game winner since Dizzy Dean in 1934. Don Drysdale pitched a record 58⅔ consecutive scoreless innings. Sub-2.00 ERAs, more typical of the war years and Dead Ball, had already won six of the ten ERA titles from 1963-67. In 1968, Cleveland's Luis Tiant registered a 1.60 ERA—a forty-nine-year low for the AL. And in the NL, Bob Gibson achieved his legendary 1.12 ERA, a sixty-year low bettered only twice in modern baseball. Eight starting pitchers, and as many prominent relievers, had ERAs below 2.00. The American League imploded with an all-time low .230 league-wide batting average. It had exactly one .300 hitter—Yastrzemski's .301 average is the lowest ever for a champion.

Enough. For 1969, rule-makers returned the strike zone to the 1950-1962 standard: armpits to the top of the knees. They also lowered the mound by a third, bringing pitchers five inches closer to Earth (though interviews with pitchers of the time indicate that the strike zone was the more significant change).

Offense gradually returned to respectability. AL expansion in 1977 added an offensive spike in the late 1970s. Throughout the 1970s and early 1980s, baseball had perhaps its best balance between offense and pitching ever. There was ample power, but the stolen base had returned, too (Lou Brock set the record with 118 steals in 1974, then Rickey Henderson topped that with 130 in 1982). Superstar starting pitchers were in rich supply and bullpens were deeper and better than ever. From 1969 to 1987, sixteen franchises played in the World Series—uncommon balance. In short, the baseball was good enough to overcome double-knit uniforms, mutton-chop sideburns, and an abundance of AstroTurf in cavernous multi-use stadiums.

But instead of leveling off, offense kept rising. Umpires were calling an even smaller strike zone than the rule book required. Strike zones had always varied by umpire, but by the mid-1980s, most strike zones were no higher than the batter's belt. The results were predictable. In 1987 a record number of home runs were hit. Mark McGwire led the AL with a rookie-record 49 homers. Don Mattingly hit homers in a record eight straight games and belted out a record six grand slams. In the NL, home runs were up 19% and batting average reached its high for the decade.

Rule-makers rewrote the strike zone in 1988 with boundaries that were "the midpoint between the top of the shoulders and the top of the uniform pants, and the lower level is a line at the top of the knees." That was still a smaller strike zone than the 1969 rule, but larger than the strike zone that had evolved on the field. Offense dropped off immediately in 1988, but started to climb again in the 1990s amid assertions that umpires were calling their own strike zones again.

Then, after the 1993 expansion, offense soared. When the 1994 season was aborted by a players strike six weeks early, Tony Gwynn was hitting .394, with a shot at becoming the first .400 hitter in more than fifty years. Matt Williams and Ken Griffey Jr. were on pace to break Maris' home-run record. Albert Belle was threatening to break Earl Webb's sixty-three-year-old record of 67 doubles in a season. Great hitting feats were everywhere and league-wide norms were reminiscent of the pre-World War II Lively Ball Era. Offense was nearly as potent in 1995.

Major League Baseball's wrestling match with umpires over the strike zone has continued ever since. In 2003 MLB installed computers in every park to evaluate the umpires' ball-strike calls. Each home-plate umpire received a computerized report after every game showing how many calls the computer said he "missed." With offense going ever higher, and home run records falling faster than a teenager's heart, MLB renewed performance expectations for umpires in 2005. Pitchers held their own in 2005, but offenses surged again in 2006, when run scoring, home runs, and batting average all rose significantly.

Hitter Parks / Pitcher Parks

The 1990s saw a slew of new construction of stadiums, most of which were hitter-friendly ballparks. Many people new to baseball assume that ballparks must follow strict standards of construction, at least where official play occurs, much like a football field or hockey rink. In reality, stadiums across the country display a variety of setups and designs. Distance to the outfield fences is just one of several things that determine whether a ballpark is pitcher-friendly or hitter-friendly. Atmospheric conditions—temperature, humidity, wind direction, altitude—also matter. The fences are a typical distance in Colorado's Coors Field, but from the day it opened in 1995 it has been Major League Baseball's best hitters' park because the ball carries a mile in mile-high altitude with low humidity. The type of infield surface makes a difference too. Artificial turf yields more hits, doubles, triples and more stolen bases because both the baseball and runners gain speed on it. Grass means more errors, because bounces are less predictable, and fewer double plays, because the ball gets to infielders slower.

Perhaps more consistently than anything else, how much foul territory a park has determines whether or not a park will be hitter friendly. Oakland's stadium, for example, has vast foul ground. It's a pitcher's park. Numerous pop fouls that would land several rows into the seats at other parks are caught easily in Oakland, denying batters another chance to get a hit or walk.

Almost all of the newer ballparks have scant foul ground. This is great for fans, who now sit much closer to the action than in the 1970s and '80s, when baseball was dominated by ballparks also used for football and other events. Hardly any of those huge, uninviting parks are left. They have been replaced by charming, baseball-only parks with fans close enough to see everything. These newer parks have been great for hitters as well.

A change in ballparks can change a player's statistical performance dramatically. Larry Walker was already a fine hitter when he played home games in Montreal, a neutral park that offered no advantage to hitters or pitchers. When he moved to Colorado and the best hitter's park in baseball in 1995, everyone expected big things from Walker. Indeed, he won three batting titles for the Rockies and twice had slugging averages above .700.

Teams tailor their talent to their ballparks' idiosyncrasies. The New York Yankees, by far the most successful team since Yankee Stadium opened in 1923, have relied on a long line of left-handed power hitters to take advantage of a right field fence much nearer to home plate than the fence in left: Babe Ruth, Lou Gehrig, Mickey Mantle, Roger Maris, Graig Nettles, Don Mattingly and Jason Giambi among them. Left-handed pitchers have the advantage here, too, so the Yankees have relied on such aces as Herb Pennock, Lefty Gomez, Eddie Lopat, Whitey Ford, Ron Guidry, Andy Pettitte and Randy Johnson.

With its left field "Green Monster" within such easy reach, Boston's Fenway Park has been a hitter's dream for generations. Counterintuitively, it is not the homer haven of lore. More balls go off that thirty-seven-foot wall than over it. Fenway inflates batting averages and doubles. Red Sox players have won twenty-five batting titles.

The Monster indisputably aids right-handed hitters. And yet, especially since World War II, the Sox' best hitters have usually been lefties—Ted Williams, Carl Yastrzemski, Wade Boggs, David Ortiz, even Pete Runnels (a two-time batting champion), Fred Lynn and Mike Greenwell. Why? Under the Monster's influence, the Sox lineups have been overwhelmingly right-handed and the opposing pitchers have been disproportionately right-handed. The Sox lefty hitters have been able to feast on that platoon advantage.

When the Brooklyn Dodgers dominated the National League from 1947 to 1956 (with seven pennants and two near misses), their powerful lineup was so heavily right-handed that they seldom opposed a left-handed starting pitcher. Roy Campanella, Gil Hodges, Jackie Robinson, Pee Wee Reese and Carl Furillo terrorized the lefties they saw. The Braves were contenders for much of that decade, but they seldom pitched their ace, lefty Warren Spahn, against the Dodgers. Spahn's few critics point out that he achieved his greatness without much work against the best team in the league. But then it is also true that the Dodgers' Duke Snider built his Hall-of-Fame credentials as the lone regular lefty hitter in a lineup that saw (almost) nothing but right-handed pitching.

The Dodgers relied first on offense to dominate the NL when they played in intimate Ebbets Field in Brooklyn. They relied primarily on superior pitching while winning seven NL pennants from 1963 to 1981 in pitcher-friendly Dodger Stadium in Los Angeles.

Once, it seemed that every ballpark had its quirky uniqueness.

Wrigley Field in Chicago has its ivy-covered walls and hitter-friendly winds (most of the time), carrying balls onto Waveland Avenue beyond a left-field power alley that is one of the most easily reached in the game's history.

The horseshoe-shaped Polo Grounds in New York had foul lines of just 280 feet in left field and a mere 258 in right, but then the outfield took right-angle turns toward a vast center field that was commuter-flight distance from home plate (more than 500 feet at one time). The Giants used pull hitters, of course (Mel Ott, Johnny Mize, Bobby Thomson, et al). They set the then-major league record with 221 home runs in 1947, and then signed Willie Mays, perhaps the best defensive center fielder ever, to cover the green ocean that passed for the Polo Grounds outfield. It was here that Mays made his legendary over-the-shoulder catch on the ball that Vic Wertz hit far, far from home plate in Game 1 of the 1954 World Series. That catch propelled the underdog Giants to a shocking four-game sweep of the Cleveland Indians, who had set the American League record with 111 wins that season.

The right field upper deck in Detroit's Tiger Stadium overhung the lower deck, creating cheap home runs for lefty batters. Washington's old Griffith Stadium had fences more than 420 feet down the line in left field, as deep there as it was to center field. Cincinnati's Crosley Field had a sloping terrace that made fly-catching adventurous for left fielders. The fences in Pittsburgh's Forbes Field were so distant and the outfield so vast that home runs were scarce there, but triples were plentiful.

Philadelphia's old Baker Bowl had a right field fence a scandalous 300 feet from home plate to the power alley and 280 down the line. Its wall was

One of baseball's most amusing stories involves Chuck Klein and that tin wall. During the 1930 season, when the sorry pitchers on the last-place Phils were getting shelled on a regular basis, pitching changes were frequent. As the story goes, during one of those delays, Klein knelt in right field and was daydreaming. The pitcher being yanked was so upset that he took the baseball and fired it against the right-field wall. Startled, Klein reacted on the belief that the game must have resumed. He fielded the ball and fired a perfect strike to second—he'd had no small amount of practice doing that during the Phils' miserable season.

made of tin and stood forty feet high—to prevent fans in homes beyond the wall from seeing the game for free. Pitchers had little chance there, but the Phillies' left-handed slugger Chuck Klein built his Hall-of-Fame caliber statistics there. Statistics like his 1930 line: .386 batting average, 59 doubles, 40 home runs, 170 RBIs, 158 runs scored.

Looking back at pitching and hitting statistics, these ballpark effects need to be taken into account. In some places with very modern statistics, you'll see the phrase, "park-adjusted." That is an attempt to adjust for the variation caused by some ballparks.

By 1959 the prevailing mood was that teams had too much of a home-field edge, that fence dimensions and other conditions were being manipulated too often to cater to the home team's talent on hand. Standards were set: After 1959, new ballparks had to be at least 325 feet down each line and at least 400 feet to the center field fence.

This prevented some shenanigans, but variation remains. Some parks, new and old, are friendlier to pitchers, some to hitters. Some are friendlier to left-handers, some to right-handers. Houston's Astrodome, which opened in 1965, was a pitcher's paradise for thirty-five years. Home runs were not part of the game plan there. In 2000 the Astros moved into their new ballpark, and it is one of the friendliest in the league for right-handed hitters.

Grass / Turf

Artificial turf changed baseball. It changed the way the game was played and who was allowed to play it. That's less of an issue now that the synthetic stuff is pretty much confined to domed stadiums, like Minnesota. In the late 1970s and all of the 1980s, nearly half the stadiums had it, creating frequent match-ups between teams tailored for turf and opponents better suited to grass.

Speed, an advantage on grass, is essential on turf. That's especially true in the outfield, where balls gain speed with each bounce. If an outfielder fails to reach the ball fast enough, hits that would have been a single on grass can easily turn into extra bases. No team understood this better than the St. Louis Cardinals, who played on turf when they were managed by Whitey Herzog in the 1980s.

After three trips to the World Series in the 1960s, the Cardinals had slipped into persistent mediocrity until Herzog took the wheel in 1981 and guided the Cardinals into the World Series in 1982, 1985 and 1987. The '87 team had only three of the lineup regulars (Ozzie Smith, Willie McGee and Tom Herr) and one pitcher (Bob Forsch) common to the '82 team. They had a different closer and a different lead RBI man each time. But all three had this in common: the swiftest outfield, and the swiftest lineup in baseball.

In each year, the Cardinals were last in the majors in homers, but twice led the NL in scoring. At or near the top of the NL in walks each season, they led the NL in on-base percentage each season, usually ranked high in doubles and triples, and led the majors in stolen bases each time. Lonnie Smith was second in the NL with 68 steals in 1982. Vince Coleman succeeded Smith in left field and led the majors with 110 and 109 steals in '85 and '87. McGee, Andy Van Slyke, Ozzie Smith, Herr and Terry Pendleton were also base stealing threats. Without homers, the Cardinals let their legs put them in constant scoring position.

The Cardinals didn't hit 100 homers in any of these seasons. They had a pathetic 67 in 1982. In 1987 the Cardinals hit 94 home runs—the only team with less than 100 and nineteen fewer than any other team. Conversely, the Cubs, a grass-field team in a division with four turf opponents, hit an NL-best 209 home runs and finished last in the NL East.

The benefit of tailoring a team to its surroundings was on frequent display during the turf era. In 1982, '85 and '87 the Cardinals reached the World Series after beating grass teams in the NL League Championship Series. At the same time, St. Louis won only one of those World Series—against the grass-fed Milwaukee Brewers in '82, but lost to the turf teams from Kansas City ('85) and Minnesota ('87).

In 1982, the Cardinals won the seven-game Series by winning all four of the games on their home turf. The Brewers were 3-0 on grass, but their much slower outfielders had trouble tracking down the Cardinals' hits in St. Louis. In 1987, the Cardinals again won all their home games. But without home-field advantage, they lost all four in Minnesota's peculiar park, where the dome lighting, the extra-springy turf, and the baggy outfield walls always bothered unfamiliar visiting teams.

NOW WHERE ARE WE?

Dead balls and lively balls, expansion, integration, strike zones, rule changes, ballpark variation—the array of these variables shows why it has been so difficult to unearth the Holy Grail of statistics—a single number that will measure a player's relative worth. It's not for lack of trying, as we will discuss later in this book.

For now, keep this in mind:

In modern baseball encyclopedias and elsewhere, you may see statistics presented as "adjusted" stats—adjusted batting average, adjusted ERA, adjusted OPS. These are statistics adjusted for the year in which they were achieved, based on the norms of that year. Adjusted statistics tell us how different from average a player's numbers are. Adjusted statistics are especially useful for comparing players from different eras.

Here's an example of how enlightening that can be.

Bill Terry, the last man to hit .400 in the National League, hit .401 in 1930, the year the entire NL hit .303. His average was 32% higher than the norm.

Carl Yastrzemski (Yaz), whose .301 average in 1968 was the lowest ever for a batting champion, hit 31% higher than the American League norm of .230 that season, the Year of the Pitcher.

Terry: .401, 39 doubles, 15 triples, 23 homers, 57 walks, 1071 OPS

Yaz: .301, 32 doubles, 2 triples, 23 homers, 119 walks, 921 OPS

Terry and Yastrzemski's OPS—on-base plus slugging—numbers are particularly noteworthy because they combine the effects of all the other statistics (batting average, walks, extra-base hits). As calculated in the *ESPN Baseball Encylopedia*, Terry's adjusted OPS was 159, or 59% better than average for the 1930 NL.

Yaz' adjusted OPS was 168.

TAKE ME OUT TO THE BALLGAME

Stats You Need to Know at the Ballpark

Baseball has long enjoyed the lowest-priced tickets of the major team sports, but at today's prices for parking, food and souvenirs, it's an event, not a routine, for a family to attend a big-league game. With infrequent visitors outnumbering the regulars at any given game, team owners see themselves in the entertainment business as much as the baseball business.

If you are a casual fan, you'll be surrounded by people like you. Those oddballs—the fans who insist on coming to the park for the baseball—are easy enough to spot. The tell-tale signs are especially evident between innings.

When the rest of the crowd is cheering for their favorite bratwurst in the sausage race, the serious fans have heads down, updating the statistics on their scorecards.

When the rest of the crowd is trying to guess which helmet is concealing the baseball in the scoreboard version of a shell game, the serious fans are checking a different part of the scoreboard—the scores of out-of-town games.

When the rest of the crowd is trying to guess the gender of the improbably costumed mascot, the serious fans are trying to figure out the baseball trivia question of the day. Was it Rogers Hornsby, Stan Musial or Tony Gwynn who led the National League in hitting six straight years? (Hornsby.)

When the rest of the crowd is singing "YMCA," the serious fans are checking out the stats of the relief pitcher taking the mound.

If this makes the serious fan sound too, well, *serious*, remember that these folks can be your best friends when the game is on. These are the fans you can turn to when an umpire confuses you by sending a runner to the next base without a pitch being thrown (balk), awards a batter first base on a pitch he swung at and missed (catcher's interference), or calls a batter out even though an infielder dropped a popup (infield fly rule). These are the fans who, because they are keeping track of how many pitches have been thrown, can explain why the manager just pinch hit for the starting pitcher who seemed to be doing just fine.

So, if you enjoy group participation, go ahead—sing, laugh at the mascot's antics, and cheer for your favorite sausage. But if you'd also like to enjoy the baseball more, there are a few fairly simple statistics that will help you feel like one of the gang with the serious fans anticipating and second-guessing the strategy on the field.

The statistics are handy—you'll find them in bright lights on the giant electronic scoreboard and possibly on a paper insert inside the glossy magazine sold as a game program. These statistics on display at the ballpark are basic: the "primary statistics" familiar (at least in name, if not in significance) to casual fans. For batters, these are the "Triple Crown" stats: home runs, runs batted in, and batting average. For pitchers, these are wins, losses, and earned run average. Add saves for relief pitchers.

BATTING STATISTICS
Batting average (BA or AVG)

Though steadily losing stature as a benchmark for evaluating a player's offensive skill, batting average has endured as the shorthand to describe a hitter's productivity and general reputation.

For more than a century, dating to the days when home runs were rare and walks were harder to come by than they are now, hitters have been labeled by their batting average. In the shorthand, "He's a .300 hitter" is high praise, referring to the standard of excellence. A .270 hitter is merely reliable, a .250 hitter is barely acceptable, and a .220 hitter has a short baseball life to live. As for the batter who comes to the plate sporting a batting average beginning with .1, he'd better be a pitcher.

Since batting average really is a three-digit percentage (.321 means getting a hit 32.1% of your at-bats), this stat is subject to wild fluctuations early in the season, when a player has had few at-bats, but minor change late in the season. By September, a player with 500-plus at-bats who gets a hit typically will improve by two batting average points (e.g. .276 to .278), while making an out will cost him one point.

IMPRESS YOUR FRIENDS · IMPRESS YOUR FRIENDS

The last .400 hitter was Ted Williams, who hit .406 in 1941. Since then, only two batters have even hit .390. Best-remembered is Kansas City's George Brett, who settled for .390 in 1980, the first time his Royals made it to the World Series. In 1994, San Diego's Tony Gwynn was hitting .394 when a players' strike in August wiped out the rest of the season.

The difference between a .300 hitter and a .250 hitter is the difference between an All-Star and a player on the way out. It could make the difference in the championship hopes for his team. But for a full-time player with 520 at-bats over the 26-week major league season, the difference between .250 and .300 is one hit per week—just one more hit each 20 at-bats. This is why perhaps the best tribute to a batter, no matter the score nor the importance of the day's game to the standings, is simply: "He never wastes an at-bat."

Home runs (HR)

Every 10 home runs puts a hitter into a new generalized category as a power hitter. Fewer than 10 homers for a regular player in a 162-game season indicates little to no power. Double figures make that player a threat to hit one out of the park, and 20 makes that player a legitimate home-run hitter. At 30, the player is regarded as a true power hitter and at 40 an elite one. Fifty is something special. Only five men in the history of the game have ever hit 60 (Babe Ruth, Roger Maris, Sammy Sosa, Mark McGwire and Barry Bonds).

However, we are currently in an era of specialized roles. Some hitters play only against right-handed pitching; some only against left-handers. Oth-

The only man ever to eclipse 60 home runs three times didn't even lead his league in homers any of those seasons. When Sammy Sosa hit what would have been a record-setting 66 home runs for the Chicago Cubs in 1998, St. Louis' Mark McGwire hit 70. The next year, Sosa hit 63 home runs, but McGwire hit 65. Then in 2001, Sosa hit 64 homers, but San Francisco's Barry Bonds set the new record with 73.

(Sosa did lead the National League in home runs twice, however—in 2000 when he hit 50 and in 2002 when he hit 49.)

ers fill in for better players. These part-time players have to be judged by ratio rather than raw totals. When your team needs a home run, look for the man who hits at least one home run for every 20 at-bats. In 2006, for instance, Cincinnati's part-time catcher, David Ross, homered 21 times in 245 at-bats, or about one in 12.

Over his first six spectacular seasons, Albert Pujols has homered once every 13.9 at-bats. Alex Rodriguez has homered at a rate of once every 14.6 at-bats for his career.

How awesome was Barry Bonds' record-setting 73 home runs in 2001? That was one every 6.5 at-bats.

Two of the greatest sluggers ever, Lou Gehrig and Jimmie Foxx, were American League rival first basemen who entered the big leagues in 1925. They have something else in common: They each drove in 100 runs or more for 13 consecutive seasons, sharing the record.

Runs Batted In (RBI)

Batting average gets the lip service. Home runs have the glamour. But among players, RBI get the respect. The milestone that separates the special RBI men from others is 100 for a season. Hack Wilson set the all-time record with 191 in 1930. No one has come within 25 of that since.

Clearly, this is a slugger's statistic, since a home run drives in all baserunners and the batter. But at least half of all homers come with nobody on base. To find the consistent run-producers, look for a ratio of more than three RBIs per home run.

OTHER THINGS TO NOTICE:

Hits

Another prestigious milestone: collecting 200 hits for a season. Ichiro Suzuki did this for a sixth straight season in 2006. Only Wee Willie Keeler (eight seasons) and Wade Boggs (seven) have longer streaks.

Extra-base hits (EBH)

It's a special season when a batter achieves 80 doubles, triples and home runs in a season. When St. Louis' Albert Pujols became the National League's Most Valuable Player in 2005, it was his third straight season with at least 80 extra-base hits. One hundred extra-base hits? Pujols reached 99 in 2004. Hank Aaron, Mickey Mantle, Willie Mays and Ted Williams never got close. But Colorado's Todd Helton has done it twice (in 2000 and 2001). Lou Gehrig did it twice (in 1927 and 1930) and Gehrig topped 80 an amazing 10 times.

Walks (W or BB)

On-base percentage is overtaking batting average in significance, but it rarely appears on scoreboards. Patience is a virtue: Players who walk often have the highest on-base percentages. Look for players whose walks are at least 10% of their total at-bats (average is 8-9%).

Stolen bases (SB) and caught stealing (CS)

Stolen bases are thrilling plays. A speedy runner's presence on first base can distract the pitcher, catcher and infielders enough to help the batter. And yet in 2006 only 85 players (fewer than one in ten) stole at least 10 bases, while 202 hit at least 10 home runs. Most players do not steal any bases in a season. They might be too slow, in the lineup for their slugging instead of their speed, or it might be that they play for slugging teams in hitter-friendly ballparks, where multi-run innings occur often enough to make the risk of an out on the bases too costly.

Speed alone is not enough. Savvy and timeliness matter. Repeated studies have shown that, on average, stolen bases produce more runs only when the baserunning thieves are successful more than two-thirds of the time. In 2006, the average success rate was 71%. So note how often a player is caught stealing before judging his effectiveness.

A smart baserunner can steal 15, even 20 bases in a season on quickness and guile. But once you see that a player has stolen 25 or more bases, you know that he is legitimately fast. Today, it takes about 60 stolen bases (in some earlier eras considerably more, in some others considerably less) to lead the league, but there are few contenders.

STAT SLANG

There are many slang terms for home runs, including the archaic "long ball" and "round-tripper." The term "four-bagger" has survived surprisingly long. Use the hipper "dinger" to create a more up-to-date impression.

In conversation, Runs Batted In or RBI is sometimes shortened to "ribbies."

If a player is hitting below .200, he might be said to be hitting "a buck-ninety" or "a buck-seventy-five," but the buck stops there. A player hitting .200 or higher simply is hitting "two-fifty" or "three-twenty."

George Brett, the Hall of Fame third baseman who hit .305 over a 21-year career from the mid-1970s through the mid-1990s, coined a phrase still popular: If you're hitting below .200, you're "below the Mendoza line." That refers to wimpy-hitting shortstop Mario Mendoza—career average .215. In the long list of Sunday statistics published by newspapers, players are ranked in order of their batting averages. In Brett's day, Mendoza's stats often were the last line published.

PITCHING STATISTICS

Wins and Losses

Like batting average for hitters, wins is the shorthand to describe the value of starting pitchers.

"He's a 20-game winner" says less about the player's actual statistics than his status as an ace of the pitching staff. A 15-game winner is a guy you want—good and reliable, but not a star. A ".500 pitcher"—a pitcher who loses as many as he wins—is what you settle for when you can't find someone better.

With 20 wins being a benchmark for a season, you can see why 300 career wins is a sure ticket to the Hall of Fame. That's the equivalent of fifteen 20-win seasons. Most of the pitchers in the Hall have not achieved 300 wins.

The pitchers who have reached 300 wins often have taken long routes.

Don Sutton won 324 games, more than most Hall of Fame pitchers, but won 20 in a season only once. His career, mostly with the Los Angeles Dodgers, was unusually long—23 years.

Greg Maddux, still active in 2006, had won 333 games for the Chicago Cubs, Atlanta Braves and Los Angeles Dodgers through the 2006 season but had won 20 only twice—and never exceeded 20. However, he won at least 15 games in a record 17 straight seasons until that streak was broken in 2005.

Warren Spahn, who won more games (363) than any left-handed pitcher in major league history, had one of the most remarkable careers for longevity. He did not win his first game until he was 25 years old, but was still winning them when he was 44. In the year he turned 35—time for many ballplayers to retire—Spahn started a string of winning 20 or more games for six consecutive seasons.

The top individual award a pitcher can win for a single season's work is called the Cy Young Award, named for the pitcher with the most wins in Major League history. Awarded to one pitcher in both the American and National Leagues, the Cy Young Award often (but not always) goes to the pitcher who won the most games in his league. Denton True Young, nicknamed "Cyclone" shortened to "Cy," won 511 games. Time tends to erase all of baseball's important records, but this one has been unchallenged since 1911 and may be the likeliest of all to remain intact.

IMPRESS YOUR FRIENDS

Warren Spahn wore the uniform number 21 for the Boston and Milwaukee Braves. In eight different seasons he won exactly 21 games.

Earned run averages (ERA)

In this statistic, lower is better. Although the serious fan will look beyond ERA for more revealing information, for more than 100 years it has been the most-trusted, stand-alone statistic to express how well a pitcher has done his job.

Standards vary by era, but the targets are these: an ERA below 3.00 for starting pitchers; elite relievers often achieve ERAs below 2.00.

Pitchers with the most victories achieve the highest honors. But the pitchers with the dominant ERA and high strikeouts earn the deepest fan adoration.

Ask statistics-minded fans about Hall of Fame pitcher Bob Gibson, and hardly a one will be able to cite how many games he won. But they will speak of his overpowering fastball, his then-record 17 strikeouts in a 1968 World Series game, and his legendary 1.12 ERA that season.

It's popular knowledge among stat lovers that Bob Gibson's 1.12 ERA in 1968 was the best ever. Except that it's not. In "modern" baseball—the period since 1901, when the American League debuted and new rules went into force—two other pitchers have had better ERAs for a season.

Mordecai "Three Finger" Brown, a Hall of Fame pitcher, had a 1.04 ERA for the 1906 Chicago Cubs, winner of a record 116 games. Dutch Leonard of the 1914 Boston Red Sox compiled the lowest ERA of all. While statistical sources disagree on how low, it was 1.01, 1.00 or perhaps even 0.96.

The Los Angeles Dodgers' Sandy Koufax excelled for only six seasons and won many fewer games than most other pitchers who are in the Hall of Fame, yet many fans say he was the best pitcher they ever saw, maybe the best ever.

In those six seasons, Koufax became the only pitcher ever to lead his league in ERA for five consecutive seasons, with such microscopic marks as 1.88, 1.74, 2.04 and 1.73 in his final four seasons. At a time when 200 strikeouts was an excellent season's work, Koufax easily topped that all six seasons, leading the National League four times and three times topping 300—setting a record with an astonishing 382 in 1965. And he won, too, leading the NL in wins with 25, 26 and 27 three of those years. Three times, in 1963, 1965 and 1966, Koufax won pitching's informal "Triple Crown"—leading his league in wins, ERA and strikeouts in the same season.

Clearly, Koufax was the most dominant pitcher of this time (1962-66). And he did it all with a badly arthritic elbow in his throwing arm. After totally dominating in 1966, Koufax became one of the rare professional athletes to retire while at the top of his game.

Saves (SV)

With each decade beginning in the 1940s, relief pitching has become more specialized. Today, almost every team employs a "closer" whose primary duty is to pitch the final inning when his team needs to preserve a narrow lead (no more than three runs). If he succeeds, the relief pitcher earns a save—the stat that has the most to say about how many millions of dollars per year that pitcher will earn.

The save, the brainchild of Chicago baseball writer Jerome Holtzman, didn't become an official statistic until 1969 and has been calculated differently at various times. Today, leading closers accumulate 40 saves or more. The record is 57, by Bobby Thigpen of the Chicago White Sox in 1990.

When Bruce Sutter was inducted into the Hall of Fame in 2006, he was the first "pure" reliever to earn the honor. Three other pitchers—Hoyt Wilhelm, Rollie Fingers and Dennis Eckersley—owe their enshrinement to their relief pitching, but all had been starting pitchers for part of their careers. Sutter is the only pitcher in the Hall never to have started a game.

STREAKS AND MILESTONES

You are probably familiar with this sort of propaganda whenever there's a big spike in the price of gas at the pump: "Over the last five years, gas prices are stable relative to inflation." Yeah? What about that 30% increase over the last seven months? And the 70% increase over the last three years? Look closely and you find that each time the propaganda flows more freely than the gasoline, the time frame keeps changing.

In recent years, baseball teams have accelerated the practice of promoting their players on ballpark scoreboards by picking out the most favorable statistical trends. This could be useful in a "who's-hot, who's-not" sort of way, except that the team doesn't broadcast when its $12-million-a-year slugger is 1-for-24 and hasn't homered in three weeks. Instead, we get an assortment of truths, half-truths, and nothing but deceptive truths.

Said slugger, whose .226 batting average is on the scoreboard, we're told, "is hitting .290 over his last 45 games." Go back far enough, and you can find a period of usefulness somewhere, all the while concealing that he has hit all of five homers with 14 runs batted in over those 45 games—this guy's killing the team.

Here's another deception: "Joe (insert any name here) has hit safely in 10 of his last 14 games." Yeah. But is he hitting well? Take those two 0-for-5s and two 0-for-4s, add six 1-for-4s, two 1-for-3s, a 2-for-3 and a 2-for-4 and it turns out that Joe is hitting .218 during this "hot streak." A player can get a hit every day for two weeks, but if it's a string of 1-for-4s, he's still hitting only .250 during his streak.

When presented forthrightly, the good news can be useful.

A hitting streak may be mentionable when it reaches 10 consecutive games, interesting when it hits 20. It won't get national attention until it reaches 30 because one of baseball's shiniest records is Joe DiMaggio's 56-game hitting streak in 1941—an achievement never seriously challenged. (But note: Not only did Boston's Ted Williams out-hit New York's DiMaggio that year, .406 to .357, Williams also hit for a higher average during DiMaggio's streak, .412 to .408.)

Here are a few of the most noteworthy streaks and single-game accomplishments that might be challenged someday at a ballpark near you:

- Most consecutive games with a home run: 8 by Yankee Don Mattingly.

- Most consecutive hits: 12 by the Red Sox' Pinky Higgins and Tiger Walt Dropo.

- Most consecutive scoreless innings pitched: 59 by Dodger Orel Hershiser in 1988, breaking the mark of 58⅔ innings by Dodger Don Drysdale twenty years earlier.

- Most strikeouts in a game by a pitcher: 20 by the Red Sox' Roger Clemens (twice), rookie Cub Kerry Wood in 1998, and Diamondback Randy Johnson.

- Most consecutive no-hitters: 2, four days apart in 1938 by Cincinnati left-hander Johnny Vander Meer. Every time a pitcher throws a no-hitter, everyone with a sense of baseball history watches to see if he can do it the next time out.

SCOREBOARD WATCHING

The casual fan might be looking at the scoreboard often to find out who is up and what he has done in his previous plate appearances today. Serious fans, even those who already know this stuff because they're keeping score themselves, will be looking at the scoreboard too, but for more detailed information:

- **Decisions by the official scorer ("scoring decisions")**
  Was that pitch that got away a wild pitch (charged to the pitcher) or a passed ball (charged to the catcher)? Was that sharp groundball that popped out of the fielder's glove an error or a hit?

- **Pitch information**
  Some scoreboards show whether the last pitch was a fastball, curve, or other pitch. Some tally the number of strikes and balls this pitcher has thrown so far today. Others display the velocity of the last pitch. For most fans, the velocity recorded by a radar gun behind home plate is entertainment. Many major league pitchers can throw fastballs at 90 mph. Some can hit 95. A very special few, such as relief pitchers Billy Wagner and Eric Gagne, have hit 100. For fans on higher alert, the velocity reveals many truths: Does this pitcher's fastball have its usual speed? Is he able to sustain it? Is he mixing speeds well to keep the batter off guard with an assortment of pitches (fastball, curve, slider, changeup)? Have we reached the point in the game where the pitcher is tiring and his velocity is falling?

● **Out-of-town scores**

Most big-league scoreboards show the scores of other games on the same day. They show the inning and the jersey number of the pitcher. Veteran "scoreboard watchers" may have an interest in many teams and in certain pitchers performing elsewhere that day. Red Sox fans are always interested in the fate of their arch-rival Yankees. Late in the season, a game elsewhere may have strong impact on the pennant-race fortunes of a team in your park. And noticing when a team has changed pitchers (the jersey number changes) can tip you off to a rally by the other team.

Scoreboard watching is another reason to buy the game program. In addition to the scorecard, and recent statistics for the teams playing at your park that day, a good program will have identifying numbers for the pitchers on out-of-town teams.

◆ ◆ ◆

The big ballpark scoreboards won't help you when you overhear certain other conversations that might confuse you. Why is that guy rooting for one Giants batter, then rooting against the next one? And what's this about the pitcher ruining his WHIP? Those would be fans in fantasy-baseball leagues. And over there: Those two guys agreeing that the shortstop is a 1, but the left fielder is a 4? They play Strat-O-Matic, the baseball simulation game.

To keep up with those guys, you'll have to read more of this book.

KEEPING SCORE

Walk through the main gate of any ballpark and you are immediately bombarded from every angle by food stands, beer carts, and souvenir shops—capitalist consumerism on overdrive. With all this competition for your attention—and your wallet—why should you keep your eyes and ears open for the wrinkled veteran vendor shouting, "Programs! Get your programs here!"

The answer is a simple grid almost always located right in the center fold: the scorecard.

Fans keeping score at the ballpark get more out of being there. They notice much more and anticipate strategy sooner than other fans. These fans will be the first to recognize that Roy Oswalt has retired eight batters in a row, or struck out three of the last four men he's faced. They are much more likely to see that Curt Schilling will have the advantage for the next three batters, but after that—just when he's going to be hitting a vulnerable pitch count—he reaches the part of the Yankee lineup that has been giving him trouble all day. They can spot when Travis Hafner is dangerous despite being hitless, because he's been pulling the ball hard today. They are alert to Ted Lilly getting into trouble, despite throwing shutout innings, because of deep pitch counts that will catch up to him sooner or later (probably sooner).

When a player has struck out three times, or gotten three straight hits on the way to a cycle, some scoreboards will tell you that when he comes up the next time. But nothing puts this into your awareness as well as writing it down yourself.

Scorekeeping has endured because it is habit-forming. Being so aware of the baseball before you is richly satisfying. Having a permanent record of a memorable game is priceless.

◆ ◆ ◆

Keeping score is as simple as you want it to be. Don't worry about doing it "right"—no two casual fans, "serious" fans, writers, broadcasters, or team officials keep score exactly alike. Everyone has his or her own codes, symbols and preferences. This chapter merely offers one suggested way to keep score. You simply need to be able to track the progress of a team's inning at-bat and to decipher your own codes later. If you can look at your scorecard two weeks after the game and still know what happened, then you've done a good job.

Here's how we'll help in this chapter:

- We'll present a basic system of keeping score, and offer you alternatives.

- We'll show how to add detail to your scorekeeping if you want that.

- We'll demonstrate by showing how Game Four of the 2006 World Series would be scored in this system.

THE SCORESHEET

Scoresheets are grids. The lineup/batting order is listed vertically along the left. Some scoresheets have a space to record each player's jersey number for easy recognition. Most have a place to record the player's fielding position (catcher, second base, etc.). Preferably, there are two or three lines for each lineup spot. That permits easy entry of pinch hitters, pinch runners, and/or defensive replacements. Innings (at least nine, usually ten to twelve) are listed horizontally across the top.

The result of this grid is a square for each inning to the right of each player's name. When a player comes up in that inning, the results of his plate appearance are recorded in that square.

On some scoresheets, those squares are blank. On others, a small diamond-shaped rectangle represents the bases the player might achieve. More detailed scoresheets might also have spaces to record balls and strikes.

THE SYMBOLS

Now it's time to record what the batter did.

We want to show whether he got on base or made an out. If he hit the ball, we want to show where it went.

Let's start with the outs.

Some scorekeepers are happy with symbols that simply show that a batter popped out (PO), grounded out (GO), flied out (FO) or lined out (LO). They will enter SAC for a sacrifice, SF for a sacrifice fly, and FC for a fielder's choice.

However, most people want to show who fielded the ball. There's a universal code for all the different positions:

1–pitcher

2–catcher

3–first baseman

4–second baseman

5–third baseman

6–shortstop

7–left fielder

8–center fielder

9–right fielder

0–designated hitter

Flyouts and popouts

When a ball is caught in the air, it's sufficient to enter the number of the fielder who caught the ball (e.g. "8" for a flyout to the center fielder). Such an entry assumes a flyout to an outfielder or popout to an infielder.

If it's a line drive, you might want to put an "L" in front of the number (e.g. "L4").

A ball caught in foul territory can be entered with a lower-case "f" (e.g. "f2").

A sacrifice fly is SF followed by the outfielder's position number (e.g. SF7).

Ground outs

When a throw is necessary to retire the batter, both the throwing fielder (who gets an assist) and the catching fielder (who gets a putout) are entered, separated by a hyphen.

Enter 6-3 for a groundball that the shortstop fields and throws to the first baseman.

Make it "DP 6-4-3" or simply 6-4-3 for a double play started by the shortstop, with a putout and relay throw by the second baseman.

Make it "FC 4-6" or simply "4-6" for a fielder's choice where the second baseman tosses to the shortstop covering for the putout.

Make it 3-1 for a groundball to the first baseman who flips to the pitcher covering first.

Make it "3u" for a groundball to the first baseman who steps on first base to record the out unassisted.

For a sacrifice bunt, make it "SAC 5-3" when the third baseman throws out the hitter at first, but it advances the runner a base.

Strikeouts

"K" is so widely recognized as the symbol for a strikeout that pitcher statistics for strikeouts are sometimes expressed as "Ks."

A swinging strikeout is a "K." A called strikeout is a "K" backwards.

Hits, walks and errors

Single = 1B

Double = 2B

Triple = 3B

Home run = HR

Walk = W or BB (IW or IBB for an intentional walk)

Hit by Pitch = HBP or HB

Error = E (followed by the fielding position of the defender; e.g. E6)

In all cases, darken (or begin to draw, depending on your scorecard) the edges of a diamond to show the player's progress on the bases.

If the batter reaches first base, simply darken the edge between home plate and first base only.

If the batter reaches second base, darken both the edge between home and first and the edge between first and second.

To locate a hit, simply add the fielding position. A single to center field becomes 1B8. An infield hit might be 1B5. If you want more specificity on balls hit into the gaps, 2B78 would indicate a double to left-center.

Variation: Some scorekeepers, seeking to avoid confusion with the numeric system for outs, avoid numbers and letters when recording hits. Instead, they use horizontal strokes—one for a single, two for a double and so on. Then, extending from the topmost stroke, another stroke showing the direction of the hit.

Progress on the bases

Each time a player advances bases on teammate at-bats, darken the edges of the diamond accordingly.

If he steals a base (SB), or advances on a balk (BK), wild pitch (WP) or passed ball (PB), also enter the code along the edge representing that advance.

Baserunners put out

When a baserunner is out, simply show it after the last base he achieved successfully.

For example, if he fails to make it to second on a fielder's choice started by the shortstop, enter 6-4 along the edge of the diamond between first and second base.

If he is thrown out at the plate by the right fielder, enter 9-2 along the edge of the diamond between third base and home plate.

If he is caught stealing third, a simple CS along the edge between second and third base will suffice.

If he is picked off first base, enter PO (or "po" if you are using PO for popout) along the edge between first and second base.

Substitutions

Enter the names of substitute players in the batting order spot where they have been placed. Usually, this is under the player they replace, but not always: Teams will sometimes make "double switches" to delay a new pitcher's time at bat.

When a batter leaves the lineup, draw a dark vertical line on the right edge of the square containing his final plate appearance.

When a pitcher leaves the game, draw a dark horizontal line at the bottom of the square of the last batter he faced (that's on the other team's lineup sheet).

Miscellaneous entries

Officially, all fielders who touch the ball in the process of recording an out are part of the play. So a groundball deflected by the pitcher that is then gloved by the second baseman who throws to first in time for the out is officially scored 1-4-3. (This is why "DP" is the preface for double plays.)

Similarly, a runner thrown out at home by the shortstop who cut off the throw from the left fielder is retired 7-6-2.

This can get messy on rundown plays where several fielders may be involved and some may handle the ball more than once.

The edge of the diamond between home and first can be used for any of several purposes:

- Some scorekeepers put the batter result here rather than in the center of the square.
- Some scorekeepers record runs batted in here. One way to do so is to write and circle the number of RBIs in that plate appearance.
- Some scorekeepers use a circled 1, 2 or 3 here to show the number of outs in the inning. Many scorekeepers don't need this assistance, but it can be useful for finding the out-makers swiftly.

Just about every scorecard also includes space to add up the total numbers of runs, hits, errors, and men left on base for each inning, as well as an area to tally the final offensive stats for each player. Most scorecards also contain a pitching chart of some sort. After a pitcher has left a game you can use this area to record his total stats—innings pitched, runs given up, earned runs, hits, walks, strikeouts, and wild pitches. At the end of a game, give the appropriate pitchers a win, loss or save.

When you have decided how you'd like to keep score, you may obtain scoresheets in several ways: download samples for free from various Internet sites, including www.baseball-almanac.com; find books of baseball scoresheets in retail stores or from the publisher of this book; copy the scoresheets that come with simulation board games such as Strat-O-Matic; or purchase a program the next time you enjoy a game at your local ballpark.

The Baseball Scorecard

Notes:	WORLD SERIES - GAME 4			Start Time:			Attendance: 46,470

■ Visitor:	DETROIT	Date: 10-26-06	End Time:		Wind: 7 mph

☐ Home:	ST. LOUIS	Scorer:	Time of Game: 3:35	Weather: 53°

#	Line Up	Pos	1	2	3	4	5	6	7	8	9	10	AB	R	H	RBI
28	GRANDERSON	8	L6		2B	K		3-4		K			5	1	1	0
27	MONROE	7	6-3		5-3		5-3		7		K		5	0	0	0
9	GUILLEN	6	K		W		1B		W 5B	F 3-4			3	1	1	0
30	ORDONEZ	9		K	7		F 8		K	6-3			5	0	0	0
21	CASEY	3		HR	1B		J		9				4	1	3	2
7	I. RODRIGUEZ	2		1B	1B		FC. 5-4			2B			4	1	3	1
14	POLANCO	4		8	FC. 6-4			7		4-3			4	0	0	0
15	INGE	5		I BB		8		1B		2B			3	0	2	1
38	BONDERMAN	1		FP		K		SAC 3-4		K			2	0	0	0
56	ROONEY	1		3U									0	0	0	0
45	GOMEZ	PH						GOMEZ					1	0	0	0
54	ZUMAYA	1											0	0	0	0

		1	2	3	4	5	6	7	8	9	10				
S	Runs	0	1	2	0	0	0	0	1	0		4
U	Hits	0	2	3	0	2	1	0	2	0		10
M	Errors	0	0	0	0	0	0	0	0	0		0
S	Left on Base	0	2	2	0	2	1	1	1	0		9

#	Pitchers	W/L/S	IP	H	R	ER	BB	SO	HB	BK	WP	TBF
38	BONDERMAN		5 1/3	6	2	2	4	4	0	0	0	25
56	ROONEY		1 2/3	2	2	0	1	4	0	0	0	8
54	ZUMAYA	L	1	1	1	1	1	1	0	0	1	5

#	Catchers	PB
7	RODRIGUEZ	

Umpires	
HP: MIKE WINTERS	
1B: JOHN HIRSCHBECK	3B: RANDY MARSH
2B: TIM McCLELLAND	

The Baseball Scorecard

Notes:	WORLD SERIES – GAME 4		Start Time:		Attendance:
Visitor:	DETROIT	Date:	End Time:		Wind:
Home:	ST. LOUIS	Scorer:	Time of Game:		Weather:

#	Line Up	Pos	1	2	3	4	5	6	7	8	9	10	AB	R	H	RBI
22	ECKSTEIN	6	FFFF 1B	2B		5-3		2B	2B			5	1	4	2
16	DUNCAN	9											2	0	0	0
99	TAGUCHI	PH, 9,7	DP 6-3	W		4-3		EI SAC	f3			1	1	0	0
5	PUJOLS	3	7		5-3	W		7-5 BB out				2	0	0	0
15	EDMONDS	8		K		4-3	F K		F 7			4	0	0	0
27	ROLEN	5		FFF 7		2B		2B	K			4	1	2	0
3	WILSON	7		F 1-3		4-3		SAC 1-3 1B				3	0	1	1
50	WAINWRIGHT	1										0	0	0	0
4	MOLINA	2			5-3 2B		W		W			2	0	1	1
12	MILES	4			SB 1B	I BB		K	FC 4 WP			3	2	1	0
37	SUPPAN	1			K	5-3		K				2	0	0	0
53	J. RODRIGUEZ	PH										1	0	0	0
52	KINNEY	1					RoDRIGUEZ		K			0	0	0	0
61	JOHNSON	1										0	0	0	0
41	LOOPER	1										0	0	0	0
43	ENCARNACION	9										1	0	0	0

S U M S		1	2	3	4	5	6	7	8	9	10	
	Runs	0	0	1	1	0	0	2	1			5
	Hits	1	0	2	2	0	1	2	1			9
	Errors	0	0	0	0	0	0	1	0			1
	Left on Base	0	0	2	2	1	2	1	1			9

#	Pitchers	W/L/S	IP	H	R	ER	BB	SO	HB	BK	WP	TBF
37	SUPPAN		6	8	3	3	2	4	0	0	0	28
52	KINNEY		2/3	0	0	0	1	1	0	0	0	3
61	JOHNSON		1/3	0	0	0	0	0	0	0	0	2
41	LOOPER		1/3	1	1	1	0	0	0	0	0	6
50	WAINWRIGHT	W	1 2/3	1	0	0	0	3				

#	Catchers	PB
4	MOLINA	0

Umpires	
HP:	3B:
1B:	
2B:	

NOW PLAYING ON A TV SCREEN NEAR YOU

If statistics were *not* the language of baseball, televised games would tell us that. Television has so many other ways to communicate—moving pictures, spoken words, game sounds—that stats would hardly be necessary, unless they *are* necessary. In fact, the stats get about as much air time as the announcers. The stats are so fundamental to game coverage that the broadcasts take it for granted that their viewers have a certain amount of preexisting knowledge.

So if you're new to baseball, a TV game can be a rapid education, or it can leave you feeling hopelessly behind, depending on your aptitude.

In this chapter we aim to make that transition painless by preparing you for what you will see and hear on TV.

We don't want to neglect radio, where stats also have an important role. But it's painful to admit this: Baseball statistics play better on television than they do on radio.

Those of us who see something much more profound in baseball's numbers than mere accounting would be more than content to link them to the aesthetic beauty of baseball on the radio. In the way that reading a book can be more fulfilling than watching the movie based on that book, listening to a baseball game on the radio can be more satisfying than watching it. In both cases, the imagination paints the more perfect picture.

Alas, when it comes to statistics, the magic of baseball on the radio is an arcane art. We might suppose that with its moving pictures and video replays, TV would rely less on numbers. But at their best, stats are seen, not heard. We all remember more of what we see than what we hear, and if a stat is not remembered, it's just a number. It ought to be more—the context that gives this at-bat and this game significance.

For a TV game, that context is more important than ever. It fuels the anticipation that keeps a viewer paying attention in twenty-first century TV's constant war with distraction.

Today's sports TV consumers are a study in adult attention deficit disorder. They're at the home computer, glancing at the TV for highlights. They're at the sports bar, sneaking peeks at the game. They might even be reading this book while the game is on. If they are watching most of the game, they almost certainly have the remote in hand and might be using the mute button while listening to U2, or the friend they just called.

Without close concentration, audio stats are a lost cause. Radio baseball requires focus to track even the most basic baseball numbers: pitch count, the runners on base, and the number of outs, among other things. To an escalating degree, TV overcomes this with graphic displays. The game-situation strip showing the score, the baserunners, the inning, the number of outs, and the pitch count is so ubiquitous today that it's easy to forget that the technique is only a few years old.

The game-situation strip outwits the mute button and solves the predicament of distracted viewers checking in for updates. These techniques also relieve the TV announcers of the duty radio announcers have to perform all the time. Legendary announcer Red Barber, who began calling Brooklyn Dodgers games before television, used to have a three-minute timer as a reminder to recite the score at least that often. Today, an adequately staffed TV game has a stats maven who feeds relevant data to the announcers and cues the producer to display prepackaged graphics prepared by a supporting cast of number crunchers.

At the same time, televised games are not the only source of stats on the small screen: Shows reviewing the day's games and statistics are fast becoming nearly as popular as the games themselves, what with their comprehensive content and hilarious on-air personalities, and they throw just as many stats at fans as the games themselves do, if not more. These fast-paced overviews require attention and demand a prerequisite understanding of statistics.

To illustrate the stats you'll need a command of to fully enjoy baseball on television, we offer a glimpse at a couple of characteristic broadcasts: a game aired on Fox Sports from the 2005 regular season and an episode of ESPN's *Baseball Tonight*. For the game, it's important to note that, during the regular season, sports announcers are much more willing to delve deeply into obscure stats than they would during a World Series game when more casual fans are viewing and the networks need to keep things simple. As for *Baseball Tonight*, there really is no watering it down: They hit the stats and they hit them hard for the entire hour of broadcast.

Stats are the language of baseball.

◆ ◆ ◆

Before the first pitch on August 27, 2005, announcers Kenny Albert and Tom Hutton have established the story line for this game between the Florida Marlins and the Chicago Cubs at Chicago's Wrigley Field. The teams might be mediocre—neither is playing like a team that expects to be in the post-season—but today's pitchers are cast as the leading men in a classic struggle between experience and youth.

The Cubs are starting Greg Maddux, the 39-year-old master whose 315 wins in 20 seasons is 16th best of all time. The Marlins answer with 23-year-old upstart Dontrelle Willis who, up to this point in his third big-league season, has won 41, including 17 this season. Both are superior athletes—they hit and run better than most pitchers and both are superior fielders. Each is a classic example of the most talented kid in the neighborhood who gets to be the pitcher.

Eight times Albert and Hutton will tell us of the statistical milestones Maddux has reached due to longevity—his 15 wins or more in 17 consecutive seasons, his 14 Gold Gloves as the league's best fielding pitcher, and, of course, his 315 wins. Eleven times they will tell us that a win today will be number 18 this year for Willis—which will tie him with Carl Pavano for the most ever in a season by a Marlins pitcher and will tie him this season with St. Louis' Chris Carpenter for the most wins in the National League.

Neither Albert nor Hutton mention it, but the story has more depth. Maddux pitches with economy of motion and precision that understate his competitiveness and cast him as the prototypical mentor. Willis is all animation—swiveling body, big leg kick, whipping pitches with the exuberance of youth. Maddux is a right-hander, Willis a lefty. Maddux is white, Willis black. This could be Anthony Hopkins teaching Antonio Banderas to be Zorro. In any case, the stage for a pitching duel is set.

Both pitchers are quick workers, and when the expected duel develops, this becomes a fast game—just two hours, twenty minutes—that involves no pinch hitters, no pinch runners, and only two relief pitchers. Given less time and less opportunity to present a deluge of statistics, Albert and Hutton overcome this obstacle with the ease of a 1-2-3 inning.

Even before Florida's Juan Pierre gets into the batter's box as the game's first hitter, the broadcast provides us with twenty-five statistics. Some have to do with the Maddux-Willis theme, but the stats set the stage with these props, too:

- A graphic shows us stats for Marlins sluggers Carlos Delgado (25 home runs, 90 runs batted in) and Miguel Cabrera (27 and 90). Hutton adds that Delgado has hit 30 homers in eight straight seasons.

- Maddux' 19 wins vs. Florida for his career is more against the Marlins than any other pitcher. He is 1-1 vs. Florida this year. He has a 2.75 ERA lifetime against Florida.

- A standard graphic any time a pitcher enters the game: A vertical stat grid showing this year's numbers for Won-Lost record (10-10), ERA (4.56), starts (27), complete games (1), innings pitched (189 2/3), hits allowed (185), walks (29) and strikeouts (104).

- Juan Pierre has a six-game hit streak, hitting .440 with 4 RBI and 8 runs in those games.

- Nomar Garciaparra is making his first start ever at third base, making him the 103rd Cub player at that position since the departure of Cub All-Star Ron Santo.

On a cloudy Saturday afternoon in Chicago, it's clear that Albert and Hutton expect a baseball-savvy TV audience. They offer no qualitative comment on any of these stats, except for Maddux' status as the number one Marlins killer. We are supposed to understand that Delgado and Cabrera are likely to reach the nice 30-homer and 100-RBI milestones, that Delgado's streak of 30-homer seasons is long, that Maddux' 2005 stats are well below his customary standards, that Pierre is suddenly very productive in a below-average season, and that Santo last played for the Cubs in 1973.

The first inning gives you a good idea of stats' role in this broadcast.

A standard batter graphic greets Pierre's first plate appearance: His season-to-date batting average (.265), home runs (2), and runs batted in (36), the Triple Crown stats. This is displayed for every batter all game. After the first time through the batting order, a second stat line shows what each batter has done so far in today's game. Albert adds a bonus for Pierre's first time up: He is "a .348 career hitter against Maddux, 8 hits in 23 at-bats."

Pierre takes first base after being hit by a Maddux pitch. Now that the game is afoot, we're immediately informed by Albert that "Pierre has 44 steals, three in the last two games after going 12 games without a stolen base." Good timing: Pierre swipes second and we learn that this theft ties him with the Mets' Jose Reyes for the NL lead at 45.

We're on alert again: Marlins number two hitter Jeff Conine had three hits yesterday and drove in three runs. When he sacrifices Pierre to third base, Maddux fields the bunt flawlessly and we're told, "When you've won 14 Gold Gloves, you're not going to mishandle that."

That brings up Cabrera. His sacrifice fly to right field, scoring Pierre, Albert notes, gives Cabrera 91 RBI for the season. The Marlins lead 1-0.

The bottom of the first starts with a weather stat: It's 77 degrees.

Then the line on Willis: "In three career starts here at Wrigley Field, Willis has allowed only two earned runs in $19\frac{1}{3}$ innings." The vertical stat graphic on Willis' season in progress:

Record	17-8
ERA	2.87
Starts	26
CG	6
Innings	$178\frac{2}{3}$
Hits	161
Walks	41
Strikeouts	124

The stats earn no comment from the announcers. You are supposed to recognize that the record, ERA, CG (for complete games) and hits-plus-walks per innings pitched are all considerably better than average.

Another graphic showing the Cubs' lineup highlights right-fielder Jeromy Burnitz. In his last seven games, he has hit .345 with 2 home runs and 10 RBI.

As leadoff hitter Jerry Hairston Jr. steps to the plate, we're told for the third time that a win today will tie Willis with Pavano for the club record with 18 wins.

Hairston grounds out so promptly that number two hitter Todd Walker is up before the broadcast can show us the graphic of the Marlins' defensive alignment. Now we know that the Marlins rank fifth defensively in the NL (though without explanation that this is determined by team fielding percentage). Curiously, though, Alex Gonzalez has committed 15 errors, the most by an NL shortstop.

There's a reason why the left-handed hitting Walker is in the lineup against Willis, who can be very tough on lefties: Walker is 2-for-3 in his career against Willis. Walker promptly singles to right.

Cubs first baseman Derrek Lee is up now. He's had a huge season. Despite going "0-for-4 yesterday with a couple of strikeouts" he's second in the NL with 37 home runs and 91 RBI. But Lee, in a mild slump, hits a routine fly out to right field.

Catcher Michael Barrett is batting fourth for the Cubs. That's unusual. "Barrett is in the cleanup spot for the third time this season," Albert notes. Baseball's team statisticians track everything. They provide a thick packet of data to all media at the game. Barrett hits a groundball to shortstop that

Gonzalez fields routinely and flips to second base for the fielder's choice that ends the inning.

◆ ◆ ◆

So far, we have many more stats than pitches. This continues for nine innings. Maddux' fortunes show us how the statistical line becomes the story line:

Second inning:

Maddux retires the Marlins 1-2-3 and Albert declares "A seven-pitch second for Greg Maddux." We're supposed to know that this is highly efficient work and a good sign that Maddux might pitch deep into this game.

Third inning:

This half-inning illustrates how stats are such a fixture in TV games that they get on the air even when the timing for presenting them is irrelevant to the game.

All this with Marlins catcher Matt Treanor at bat:

A graphic shows that Maddux' 315 wins places him 16th all-time and that Phil Niekro, who is number 15, has 318. Among active pitchers, Maddux trails only Roger Clemens.

However, Albert adds, "Over his last 11 starts, Maddux has gone just 3-6."

Tom Glavine, who pitched for years as Maddux' teammate in Atlanta, is pitching for the Mets now. He's going for win number 273 today in San Francisco. Maddux won his 300th game in San Francisco last August. Ah, the point: Since 1991, Maddux has won the most games—255—and Glavine is number two.

None of this has anything to do with Treanor. Remember, Maddux and Willis are the leading men in this show.

This continues with the Cubs at bat in the bottom of the third inning. With top Cubs hitter Lee up, the camera switches to a close-up of Maddux in the dugout. Now we learn that he is "the all-time leader in putouts by a pitcher." This is about as obscure as stats get. Any fan who cares about pitcher putouts has been well concealed.

Fifth inning:

We are alerted that since Juan Encarnacion's single, the Marlins' only hit so far, Maddux has retired eight batters in a row. Oops. Encarnacion drills a double to left field. Easley follows with a bunt between the pitching mound and third base. Maddux is on it decisively with intent to throw to third. But Garciaparra is not prepared and both runners are safe. It's Garciaparra's first game as a third baseman, the announcers remind us, after playing 1,024 games at shortstop.

It's a tough spot for Maddux—runners at first and third and none out. He gets Gonzalez to pop out. The broadcast producers then twice interrupt the tension building in this inning.

First, they decide to show a video highlight from St. Louis, where part-time outfielder So Taguchi has hit a two-run single to put the Cardinals ahead. We're told that Taguchi "now has 44 RBIs," as if this ordinary number achieved by a minor player is anything but meaningless at this late stage of the season.

Then we get a graphic that had its place last inning alongside an interview with Marlins Manager Jack McKeon, who is nearing his 1,000[th] win:

MOST MANAGERIAL WINS

1. Connie Mack   3,731
2. John McGraw   2,763
3. Tony La Russa   2,195
    (25 years as manager)
4. Sparky Anderson   2,194
5. Bucky Harris   2,157

Finally back to the action. Maddux might be able to get out of this jam. He has to face the weak-hitting Treanor and the pitcher, Willis. A graphic shows that Maddux has thrown 19 balls, 35 strikes, and 54 pitches. We're not told anything more about this stat, but it could have been explained this way: That's good command, but not extra special. Any pitch swung at is counted as a strike, even if it was out of the strike zone and even if it is hit for a home run. So the strikes should always be much higher than the balls.

Maddux, whose control usually is impeccable, walks Treanor to load the bases with one out. Then he hits Willis with a pitch to force in a run that puts the Marlins ahead, 2-1. A graphic shows us that Willis has just moved into second place this season for runs batted in by a pitcher. It's not explained, but yes, that's a run "batted" in when a walk or hit batsman forces in a run.

Sixth inning:

The broadcast team—announcers, producer and stat-crunching support staff—has struggled to wedge all the stats into relevant places so far, but they are at their best in the top of the sixth inning.

With the game more than half over now, it's possible that Maddux' uncharacteristic control trouble last inning could be his undoing in an otherwise well-pitched game. Hutton and Albert are all over that, and they've got the numbers to drive home the irony.

Hutton notes that Maddux has hit two batters today, and both have figured in the Marlins' two runs. He also tells us that "Maddux had a stretch of $72\frac{2}{3}$ innings back in 2001 where he did not walk a batter." That remarkable number received much attention then.

Albert: "Maddux has walked one Marlin today. He does not have a strikeout. During his Major League career, he is 13th on the all-time strikeout list with 3,020; 147th on the all-time walks list, with only 900 walks."

The Marlins' Cabrera then rakes Maddux for a double and the broadcast team alertly displays this graphic that showcases the NL's top hitters in 2005, two of whom are playing in this game:

	Derrek Lee	Albert Pujols	Miguel Cabrera
TRIPLE THREAT			
AVG	.350	.334	.334
HR	37	35	27
RBI	91	98	91

Last Triple Crown: Carl Yastrzemski, 1967

Then, with Delgado at the plate, Hutton enhances the pregame stat: "Eight straight years of 30 or more home runs. Only eight players have ever done that for nine straight years."

Albert: "Barry Bonds is the record holder: He did it for 13 consecutive seasons."

Delgado is out on a called third strike and Albert is quick to point out that this is Maddux' first strikeout of the game.

With two out and Cabrera on second, Albert sets the stage for another key moment by pointing out that the next batter, Encarnacion, has two of the three Marlins hits off Maddux today. During this at-bat, the announcers observe that the velocity of Maddux' fast ball is in the mid-80s. Not impressive. But in classic Maddux fashion, Encarnacion grounds out to end the Marlins' threat.

Eighth inning:

Albert observes that Maddux' mere two strikeouts today is at odds with the fact that Cubs pitchers have led the league in strikeouts the last four years. On the other hand, one toss into the eighth inning, Maddux has thrown 88 pitches. None of the rest of this is explained to you: Apparently, if you are watching TV baseball on a summer Saturday afternoon, you are supposed to know that 100-110 pitches are the threshold for thinking about a relief pitcher. You are supposed to understand that Maddux' current pitch count makes him a candidate to complete this game. And if you remember his pregame stat grid showing just one complete game all season, that would be noteworthy.

Pierre steals third base with two out and Cabrera, the team's most reliable RBI man, at the plate—questionable strategy made more suspect when

Albert notes that "Juan Pierre has regained the NL lead with his 46th stolen base." As he adds that the theft gave Pierre five steals in the last three games, a timely graphic appears.

MOST STOLEN BASES / N.L. THIS SEASON	
J. Pierre, FLA	46
J. Reyes, NY	45
R. Furcal, ATL	38
W. Taveras, HOU	31
R. Freel, CIN	29

Hutton excuses what looks like stat-conscious selfishness by Pierre on that last steal: "The Marlins have to manufacture runs, because over their last 21 games, they've hit just six home runs, four by Carlos Delgado, two by Miguel Cabrera." In fact, the Marlins' first run today was scored without benefit of a hit in the inning and the second crossed the plate on a hit batter.

Sure enough, Cabrera grounds out and the Marlins have another zero on the scoreboard.

Ninth inning:

Maddux dispatches the Marlins easily and it's noteworthy: "Maddux goes nine."

Bottom of the ninth inning:

Is Maddux going to win this game? Not unless the Cubs rally. Willis pitched just as well, and though he left in the eighth inning after throwing his 106th pitch, the Marlins lead 2-1 and Willis will get the win if the score doesn't change.

If there's going to be a time when pure baseball will trump the parade of statistics, it's now.

Not a chance.

A graphic shows the Marlins with a chance to improve their position in the NL East standings and something more—all the teams in this division have winning records.

"This is the latest date in NL history where an entire division was above .500," Albert informs us. "It happened once in the American League."

Marlins closer Todd Jones has been wearing a Fox microphone while in the bullpen, but now that he's in the game, the microphone wired to him is silent. His stats speak for him:

Record	1-4
ERA	1.05
Saves	30
Games	54
Innings	58
Hits	41
Walks	12
Strikeouts	49

Again, it's left for you to decipher. Despite the losing record (not uncommon for closers who inherit leads and therefore can seldom win their games), Jones has otherwise impressive numbers.

Garciaparra strikes out, but Burnitz doubles off the glove of first baseman Conine, who has just moved there this inning for better game-preserving defense. When Neifi Perez hits a fly to left for the second out, Albert notes that "Todd Jones has thrown seven pitches in the inning, for seven strikes."

The Cubs' last chance resides with the weak-hitting Corey Patterson and the odds favor the Marlins. Patterson is 0-for-3 today, 1-for-5 lifetime against Jones.

Hutton: "One of the things that got Corey Patterson sent to the minors this year: 95 strikeouts, just 19 walks."

Now, hundreds of stats into this game, it's time for Albert to thank the production crew and two men for "crunching the numbers for us today for Jeff Charboneau here in the booth."

That is not a signoff on stats, however.

Time to remind us that "Todd Jones has 30 saves, 20 in a row including here at Wrigley yesterday" and that Willis allowed a run on six hits in 7⅓ innings.

Finally, Patterson's weak grounder to Conine at first base ends the game and we get a double signoff, first orally:

"Dontrelle Willis has tied Carl Pavano... and Chris Carpenter for the lead ..."

Then graphically—today's scoreboard, headlined:

Willis' 18th win, tied for most in NL this season	
Marlins	**2-5-0**
Cubs	**1-7-0**
WP:Dontrelle Willis (18-8)	
LP: Greg Maddux (10-11)	
SV: Todd Jones (31)	

BASEBALL TONIGHT

At 10:30 on a Saturday night people all over America are sitting entranced in front of movie screens, dodging flashing lights on dance floors, and savoring their best meal of the week in restaurants. But on this Saturday night, just a week before October Baseball, fans in hundreds of thousands of homes are sitting entranced in front of their television sets, keeping pace with fast talk and flashing graphics, and savoring the statistics feast known as *Baseball Tonight*.

The ESPN show ostensibly is about all matters baseball, heavy on video highlights and rapid-fire banter between a host, a former ballplayer, and a baseball journalist, showcasing today's games.

It's all a disguise. This is a show where tonight's talent—host Rece Davis, former big-league pitcher Jeff Brantley, and scribe-turned-talking-head Tim Kurkjian—get their street cred with guys who hang around street corners jazzing on statistics. Well, maybe guys whose date on a Saturday night is their home computer.

Statistics will so dominate the next sixty minutes that the numbers will get as much air time as the video. Stats from today's games will be used to transport us to the 1930s, 1940s, 1950s, 1960s, 1970s and 1980s. Stats will be spoken or shown, on average, once every six seconds (after subtracting the time for a half dozen commercial breaks). That's nearly 500 statistics in all—not including the scores of the games. *Baseball Tonight* has batting stats, pitching stats, fielding stats, attendance stats. Stats will be the reason for Davis, Brantley and Kurkjian to drop the names of today's big stars—Barry Bonds, Alex Rodriguez, Mark Teixeira, Andruw Jones—and of trendy young players like Jimmy Rollins, Jeff Francoeur and Grady Sizemore. Some of them will be compared to Joe DiMaggio, Paul Molitor and Benito Santiago, who never set their spikes in most of today's stadiums.

To fans schooled in the lyrics, this is music to the ears, with a beat and rhythm. It's as natural as singing along with a favorite tune, albeit rap, rock or heavy metal. The seldom-interrupted flurry of numbers requires full concentration from the most fluent fan. If you don't speak stats, you've got as much chance of keeping up as getting Jay-Z to invite Yanni in for keyboards on the next CD.

Why shouldn't the ESPN boys be crankin' it up? It's September 24, 2005. Pennant races are rockin'. Statistical milestones are shakin'. And thirty big-league teams are playin', with three games on the West Coast still in motion.

5, 4, 3, 2, 1....

Right "Out of the Box," as the ESPN team calls their preview segment, we hear about Alex Rodriguez' 46th home run. Jimmy Rollins has hit in his 29th straight game—only 39 times in history has anyone reached 30. Craig Biggio's 24th home run has pennant-race implications. And Barry Bonds, with 708 career home runs, was in uniform at Coors Field in Denver, where Bonds has always thrived in the most hitter-friendly stadium in baseball.

Stay tuned.

First, we're taken to the South Side of Chicago, where the White Sox have beaten the Twins to strengthen their hold on first place in the American League Central division. Video shows Minnesota's Michael Cuddyer hitting into a 6-4-3 double play, one of four twin-killings of the day. Chicago's Jermaine Dye hit his 30th homer and a full-screen graphic scoreboard with thirty stats shows that the Sox have won two in a row for the first time since early

September. For Freddy Garcia, one of the Sox starting pitchers who were 21-4 in their first 35 games, it's his first win since September 2.

Now to Kansas City, where the Sox' main competition, Cleveland, has won to keep pace. Shortstop Jhonny Peralta hit his 23rd homer of the season, a nice total for a shortstop, and Grady Sizemore hit his 22nd—a very nice total, as Brantley observes, for a leadoff hitter. It's a sign of the power in the young Indians' lineup—they hit four out today, but none by Travis Hafner, who did not hit a homer for the first time in seven games. First baseman Ben Broussard had three doubles and four RBI, though. Winning pitcher Kevin Millwood, the AL's ERA leader, gave up seven hits in six innings pitched, but only one earned run. A scoreboard with thirty-three stats tells more.

It's clear that these stat-intensive scoreboards target fantasy-league players. In addition to the score, the winning/losing pitchers and the big hitters for the day, the boards show even the 0-for-3 with 1 walk of other key players in the lineup. Each starting pitcher's stat line (innings pitched, hits allowed, earned runs allowed, walks allowed, strikeouts) is here. It's not quite as complete as a newspaper box score, but it's a highly useful account of the game at a glance.

We're now seven minutes—and 85 stats—into the show. Time to catch our breath, er, go to the first commercial.

◆ ◆ ◆

The whole hour passes this way—video trips from stadium to stadium, stat-filled graphic scoreboards, and the announcers fast-talking to squeeze more data into tiny sound bites.

At Yankee Stadium, *Baseball Tonight* has a film clip and news you won't get anywhere else—it's the third time this month Yankee pitcher Jaret Wright has been hit with a batted ball. This gets slightly higher billing than Rodriguez' 46th home run, which ties him with Joe DiMaggio for the most homers ever by a right-handed hitting Yankee. Like Rodriguez, DiMaggio did it in his second season as a Yankee, 1937.

The attraction in Colorado is Barry Bonds, who is ever closer to passing Babe Ruth in lifetime home runs. Lifetime against Rockies starter Sunny Kim, Bonds is 2-for-2 with two home runs. Here's a video highlight from a Bonds at-bat tonight. He swings and—he grounds out to second. Bonds went 0-for-3 tonight, the Rockies won 6-0, and that's all we need to tell you about this game between two bottom feeders. Here's a twenty-six-stat scoreboard if you must know more.

Thanks to stats, the *Baseball Tonight* crew can create urgency in otherwise meaningless games. The Milwaukee Brewers have reached a .500 record (77-77) with eight games to go, thanks to a seven-run second inning that chased Cardinals starting pitcher Mark Mulder in the shortest outing of his career. Kurkjian: The last time the Brewers finished a season .500 was 1992.

In a who-cares game, the New York Mets beat the Washington Nationals. Bet you didn't know this: Nationals pitcher Livan Hernandez hit a triple off Tom Glavine tonight. It's Hernandez' second triple of his career—and both have been off Glavine.

The daily treat you've been waiting for: The list of "Today's Home Runs," with a few golden nuggets of context:

● David Wright's second career grand slam makes him 7-for-13 lifetime with the bases loaded.

- Francoeur's homer was his first since September 3.

- Andruw Jones' 51st home run was his first in eight games: Kurkjian: "50 home runs for a center fielder: Mays, Mantle, Griffey and Andruw Jones."

- Rodriguez' home run ties DiMaggio's mark.

- Teixeira's homer was Texas' 257th this season.

- Ron Belliard became the ninth Cleveland player with at least 15 homers this season. That had never been done before. Now, two teams have: Cleveland and Texas.

One last commercial break, followed by the show's shortest segment, but a sweet one: video highlights of today's Web Gems—the day's top defensive plays. This is the only segment of the show where video gets more air time than stats, but the show's signoff is in numbers:

The last time both leagues had hit streaks as long as 29 games was 1987, when Paul Molitor (39-game streak) and Benito Santiago (34) did it.

The Yankees have now eclipsed four million in attendance. Only two teams—Colorado and Toronto—have done that previously. From 1951 to 1974, Kurkjian adds, the Yankees never drew more than two million fans.

And that's a wrap, at 11:30 p.m. Eastern Time. The next show is one hour from now, when, presumably, we'll have final scores from the West Coast.

That's *Baseball Tonight*.

HOW TO READ
A BOX SCORE

Despite being
published in
the smallest
type and squeezed into
narrow spaces, the baseball
box score has earned enduring respect.
Even as newspapers have gotten smaller over the years, they
have not sacrificed the box score to make space. Every web site chronicling
baseball games includes box scores too. This translation of a baseball game
into almost nothing but numbers provides fans with a concise, universal
language to relate the events of a game.

   Although the content of box scores has evolved, these grids have been
a staple of game recaps since the 1850s. As baseball statistics have become
more widespread in their use, so too has the box score widened.

The earliest box scores were mostly concerned with runs scored and outs. In modern baseball, the staples have been a lineup and four columns showing each batter's at-bats (AB), runs (R), hits (H), and runs batted in (BI). Some box scores still appear that way, but today's "expanded" box scores also have a column for season-to-date batting averages (Avg), and possibly even columns for walks (BB), strikeouts (SO), and men left on base (LOB).

Below that, the pitching grid traditionally contains columns for each pitcher's innings pitched (IP), hits allowed (H), runs allowed (R), earned runs allowed (ER), walks, (BB) and strikeouts (SO). Expanded box scores now have columns for number of pitches thrown (NP) and season-to-date earned run averages (ERA).

The information between the batting and pitching grids has also expanded, lengthening the box score with a wealth of detail on batting, baserunning, fielding and pitching.

As the box scores are crammed with ever more information, words get abbreviated—player names get condensed, entries like "three-base hits" have been shortened to "3B." But the numbers are sacred—none get removed, more get added.

Saying you are a baseball fan but don't read box scores is kind of like saying you are Christian but don't read the Bible. Like the Bible, it is never too late to begin reading box scores. Unfortunately, those who publish box scores take their readers' knowledge for granted—the boxes seldom appear with a code explaining all the abbreviations.

We can best teach you how to read a box score by showing you one.

On page 124 is the box score of the New York Mets' 5-2 victory over the Atlanta Braves on April 28, 2006. It was produced by the Associated Press and published widely in American newspapers. We chose it because this game was typical, not extraordinary, yet enough went on in this game to show you most of what you will encounter by reading box scores of many games.

In fact, the amount of information this box score reveals tells us precisely how this game was decided in a dramatic bottom of the ninth inning.

◆ ◆ ◆

The placement of the New York lineup at the top tells us that the Mets were the visitors and the Braves were at home.

This is an expanded box score. In addition to the columns for AB, R, H, BI, we have others for BB, SO and Avg.

The line for New York's leadoff hitter, Jose Reyes, shows that he played shortstop (ss), had four at-bats, scored two runs, had two hits, had one run batted in, walked once, struck out once and, after this game, was hitting .253 for the season. Because two hits in four at-bats is a .500 average, we know that he had been hitting less than .253 before the game.

We see an orderly New York lineup: Eight batter-fielders followed by the pitcher, Pedro Martinez. Most names are printed last-name-only. Those displayed with a first initial are those who have the same last name of another player in the league.

After "PMartinez," we see more players, led by the entry, "a-JuFranco ph."

That's Julio Franco. We need "JuFranco" because there's another JFranco in the league, John Franco. The "ph" tells us Franco was a pinch hitter today, and because his name appears directly beneath Martinez, we know that's

Mets 5, Braves 2
New York

	AB	R	H	BI	BB	SO	Avg.
Reyes ss	4	2	2	1	1	1	.253
Lo Duca c	4	0	2	0	0	2	.294
CDelgado 1b	3	0	0	1	1	1	.326
Wright 3b	3	2	2	3	1	1	.329
Floyd lf	4	0	1	0	1	0	.191
Nady rf	4	0	1	0	0	1	.314
KMatsui 2b	4	1	2	0	0	0	.345
Chavez cf	4	0	1	0	0	1	.233
PMartinez p	3	0	0	0	0	3	.083
a-JuFranco ph	1	0	0	0	0	0	.364
Sanchez p	0	0	0	0	0	0	.000
BWagner p	0	0	0	0	0	0	—
Totals	**34**	**5**	**11**	**5**	**4**	**10**	

Atlanta

	AB	R	H	BI	BB	SO	Avg.
MGiles 2b	4	0	0	0	0	0	.203
Renteria ss	4	0	1	0	0	1	.357
CJones 3b	4	1	1	2	0	2	.273
AJones cf	3	0	1	0	0	1	.286
LaRoche 1b	2	0	0	0	1	1	.214
1-Orr pr	0	0	0	0	0	0	.194
Remlinger p	0	0	0	0	0	0	—
Reitsma p	0	0	0	0	0	0	—
b-Diaz ph	1	0	0	0	0	1	.192
Francoeur rf	4	0	1	0	0	0	.193
McCann c	3	0	0	0	0	1	.290
c-Pratt ph	1	0	0	0	0	1	.200
Langerhans lf	3	0	1	0	0	0	.284
Smoltz p	1	1	1	0	0	0	.143
BJordan	1	0	0	0	0	0	.250
Totals	**31**	**2**	**6**	**2**	**1**	**8**	

New York	100	110	002—5	11	0
Atlanta	000	002	000—2	6	1

a-grounded into double play for PMartinez in the 8th. b-struck out for Reitsma in the 9th. c-struck out for McCann in the 9th.

1-ran for LaRoche in the 7th.

E—Francoeur (2). LOB—New York 9, Atlanta 5. 2B—Lo Duca (5), AJones (4). 3B—Reyes (3). HR—CJones (2), off PMartinez; Wright 2 (5), off Reitsma, Smoltz. RBIs—Reyes (11), CDelgado (20), Wright 3 (18), CJones 2 (10). SB—Reyes (11), KMatsui (1). CS—Francoeur (2). S—Lo Duca, Smoltz. SF—CDelgado, Wright. GIDP—JuFranco.

Runners left in scoring position—New York 6 (Reyes 2, Lo Duca, Nady 3); Atlanta 4 (MGiles, LaRoche, Pratt 2).

DP—Atlanta 1 (Remlinger, Renteria and BJordan).

New York	IP	H	R	ER	BB	SO	NP	ERA
PMartinez (5-0)	7	4	2	2	1	5	108	2.94
Sanchez	1	0	0	0	0	0	11	0.00
BWagner (6)	1	2	0	0	0	3	27	0.75
Atlanta	**IP**	**H**	**R**	**ER**	**BB**	**SO**	**NP**	**ERA**
Smoltz (1-2)	7	8	3	3	4	10	122	4.09
Remlinger	1	1	0	0	0	0	7	3.68
Reitsma	1	2	2	2	0	0	18	6.48

IBB—off Smoltz (CDelgado) 1. HBP—by BWagner (AJones). T—2:39. A—45,389 (50,091).

who he pinch hit for. The "a-" is explained below the team lineup: "grounded into double play for PMartinez in the 8th," meaning the 8th inning.

The next two names belong to pitchers: Duaner Sanchez and Billy Wagner. They didn't bat, but as soon as they entered the game, they were officially in the lineup. We can check the pitching grid at the bottom of this box score to see when they pitched and what they did. But let's wait for that while we follow the box from top to bottom.

Next is the Atlanta lineup and it looks much different from the orderly New York lineup. The Braves used many more players and at some point the batting order was scrambled. A good box score, like this one, can help us figure out when and how this happened.

We can confidently suppose that pitchers Mike Remlinger and Chris Reitsma were not in the original lineup batting seventh and eighth. Aside from the problem of having two pitchers start the game, we know by looking at the pitching grid below that Remlinger and Reitsma did not start the game at all—they relieved starting pitcher John Smoltz, who pitched seven innings. We also see that the lineup entry "1-Orr pr" is translated this way: "1-ran for LaRoche in the 7th." So we know that Pete Orr pinch ran for first baseman Adam LaRoche after LaRoche, batting fifth in the lineup, reached base in the 7th inning. Finally, we note that Orr did not play a fielding position; he was only "pr." LaRoche's replacement at first base appears at the bottom of the grid: Brian Jordan batted in the ninth place of the batting order, the spot Smoltz once held.

Now we know exactly what happened: After Orr pinch-ran and the Braves were retired in the 7th, Atlanta Manager Bobby Cox replaced both LaRoche and Smoltz. But Smoltz' position in the batting order would be the first of those two to come up and Cox did not want a pitcher batting there. So he put Jordan in that spot and put Smoltz' pitching replacement, Remlinger, in LaRoche's spot. This not only got Jordan to the plate sooner, but gave Cox the option of keeping Remlinger in the game longer instead of having to pinch hit for him in the 8th.

In addition, now we know the original lineup following LaRoche: Jeff Francoeur batted sixth, Brian McCann seventh, Ryan Langerhans eighth, with Smoltz ninth.

Next is the linescore. It tells us how many runs each team scored in each of the nine innings of this game, grouped into three groups of three innings. New York held a 3-0 lead, and Atlanta made it close with two runs in the 6th inning, but the Mets stretched their lead to 5-2 with two runs in the 9th inning. Following the inning-by-inning account in the linescore are three traditional numbers for each team—the total runs, hits and errors (the Mets had five runs, eleven hits and no errors).

The middle section of the box score tells us about notable events in the game—errors, extra-base hits, stolen bases, double plays and much more.

Here's a primer on the abbreviations and terms in box scores:

E—errors

LOB—men left on base (on the final out each inning)

2B—doubles

3B—triples

HR—home runs (who hit them and which pitchers they victimized)

RBIs—runs batted in

SB—stolen bases

CS—caught stealing

S—sacrifices (bunts)

SF—sacrifice flies

GIDP—grounded into double plays

Runners left in scoring position—runners stranded at second and third base on the final out each inning

Runners moved up (not in this box score)—the batters who advanced runners to second or third base while making outs

DP—double plays turned by the defensive team (and which defensive players recorded assists and putouts in the order that the ball was handled)

In each case where a number appears in parentheses, that is the season-to-date total in that category for that player. In this game, Francoeur, for example, committed his second error, David Wright's two home runs give him five for the season, Reyes collected his 11th RBI and stole his 11th base.

Next is the pitching grid. The pitchers for each team are shown in order of appearance.

The numbers in parentheses next to some pitchers' names reveal the winning and losing pitcher and whether the closing (final) reliever on the winning team was credited with a save. We see that Pedro Martinez won to make his season record 5-0 and Mets closer Billy Wagner recorded his sixth save of the season. Atlanta starting pitcher Smoltz was the losing pitcher, his second loss against one victory.

Each pitcher has a column to show his IP, H, R, ER, BB, SO, NP, and ERA. This data tells us how well each man pitched, and it will help us reconstruct this game without reading a game summary. So will the information below the pitching grid.

IBB abbreviates intentional walk. HBP means hit by pitch—Mets pitcher Wagner hit Andruw Jones.

T indicates how long the game took to play (2 hours, 39 minutes).

A indicates attendance—45,389 witnessed this great game. The number after that in parenthesis (50,091) is the seating capacity in Atlanta.

We know it was a great game because this box score reveals much more than statistics. It tells us this was a close game with a dramatic finish. With nothing more than the box score, we can confidently write this detailed account.

◆ ◆ ◆

New York Mets vs. Atlanta Braves, April 28, 2006

New York survived its struggle to drive in men in scoring position with two outs (six men stranded on second and third base) in this duel between Pedro Martinez and John Smoltz. The Mets led 3-0, scoring one run on a solo homer by David Wright and another on Wright's sacrifice fly. The lead was trimmed to 3-2 in the 6th, when Atlanta's Chipper Jones hit a two-run homer off Martinez.

After Smoltz and Martinez pitched scoreless seventh innings, they were done for the day. Smoltz had struggled, yielding eight hits and four walks in seven innings. After Smoltz threw 122 pitches, manager Cox knew he had little left, so he replaced him without even pinch hitting for him.

Martinez pitched well, allowing just four hits and one walk. But after five shutout innings, he gave up the homer to Chipper Jones, and by the end of the seventh Martinez had reached 108 pitches. When it was his turn up in the

8th inning, Manager Willie Randolph had an easy call—pull a tiring Martinez in favor of right-handed hitting Julio Franco to face the lefty pitcher Mike Remlinger. Maybe Franco could drive in the man on base to give the Mets something better than their 3-2 lead.

Didn't happen. Franco hit into a double play. But Mets reliever Duaner Sanchez shut down Atlanta 1-2-3 in the bottom of the 8th inning and New York got its cushion with two runs in the 9th, one scoring on Wright's second solo homer of the game.

The Mets' new 5-2 lead sure relieved some Mets fans' anxiety when Atlanta rallied in the bottom of the 9th. Edgar Renteria singled to lead off the inning against Mets closer Billy Wagner. After Chipper Jones struck out, Andruw Jones was hit by a pitch. Wagner then struck out pinch hitter Victor Diaz, but Jeff Francoeur singled to load the bases. Wagner earned the uneasy save when he struck out pinch hitter Todd Pratt with the bases loaded to end the game.

◆ ◆ ◆

How do we know all this? Everything is there in the numbers.

We could start in several places, but let's figure the pitching first. We know that each pitcher in this game threw complete innings—none shows "1/3" or "2/3" in their IP columns. Further, if any had started a new inning but failed to record an out before being replaced, we would see an entry below the pitching grid that goes something like this: "Remlinger pitched to 2 batters in the 8th." No such language appears, so we know that Martinez pitched exactly seven complete innings, Sanchez pitched the 8th, and Wagner pitched the 9th. Similarly, Smoltz went seven, Remlinger pitched the 8th, and Reitsma the 9th.

Now for the Wright stuff: He is a key figure in this game, hitting two home runs and driving in three runs. We know both homers were with no one on base because Wright also hit a sacrifice fly. Each of these plays scored one run. We also see that one of Wright's homers came off Smoltz and the other off Reitsma, so one of the solo homers was in the 9th inning.

That means the Mets' 3-0 lead involved one of Wright's solo homers and his sacrifice fly. We are sure the other home run did not happen in the first inning, because Wright batted fourth and the Mets scored only one run that inning. If Wright had slammed a dinger then, it would have been with at least one man on base.

The Braves scored only in the sixth inning, so Chipper Jones' home run happened then. Since Jones drove in both Braves runs, we know that it was a two-run homer. He couldn't have driven in a run in any other inning.

In the top of the 8th, we're informed, Franco hit into a double play. Remlinger, who pitched that inning for the Braves, allowed just one baserunner, on a hit.

In the bottom of the 8th, Sanchez allowed no baserunners. We know it was a 1-2-3 inning for him.

In the 9th, as we determined above, Wright hit his second solo homer. Unless something rare and unexplained happened, Carlos Delgado drove in the other Mets run that inning with a sacrifice fly that scored Reyes. (Having accounted for Wright's two runs and his three RBI, we know that Reyes' RBI could not have scored anyone but Kaz Matsui and, therefore, Reyes scored on sacrifice flies by Delgado and Wright.)

We can reconstruct the fascinating bottom of the 9th by working backwards.

We see that Pratt had just one plate appearance, as a pinch hitter who struck out in the 9th. We also read that he stranded two runners in scoring position, so we know he made the final out. There's another way to be sure Pratt made the final out: Every spot in the Atlanta batting order had four plate appearances (at-bats + walks + HBP + sacrifices) except for Langerhans and the Smoltz/Jordan spot. So the Braves went three complete times through their lineup and ended the fourth time through with the McCann/Pratt spot.

Reconstructing the rest of the 9th, we see that Mets closer Wagner—who pitched only the 9th—allowed two hits and struck out three batters. He also hit Andruw Jones with a pitch. So Wagner faced six men.

Working backwards from Pratt, we see that Wagner faced Pratt, Francoeur, Diaz, Andruw Jones, Chipper Jones and Renteria.

Who got the two hits? It had to be Renteria and Francouer because Chipper Jones' one hit was his homer in the sixth. Andruw Jones had a hit, but it couldn't have been in the 9th, when he was hit by Wagner's pitch.

The pitching grid tells us that all three outs Wagner recorded were strikeouts. Who struck out? We know about Pratt and we're also told that Diaz "struck out for Reitsma in the 9th." That leaves Chipper Jones, since he got on base only once and that was his homer in the 6th.

Finally, we know that Renteria's and Francouer's hits were singles, or their names would show up in the list of extra-base hits.

So now we know how the bottom of the 9th panned out: Renteria singled. Chipper Jones struck out. Andruw Jones was hit by a pitch. Diaz, pinch hitting for pitcher Reitsma, struck out. Francoeur singled, but didn't drive in a run, so the bases were loaded. Then Atlanta manager Cox chose Pratt, a right-handed hitter, to pinch hit for the lefty-hitting McCann against the lefty-pitching Wagner. But Pratt struck out with two men in scoring position and the potential tying run on base.

Those tiny numbers tell big stories.

THE POWER OF IMAGINATION

Fantasy Baseball and Simulation Games

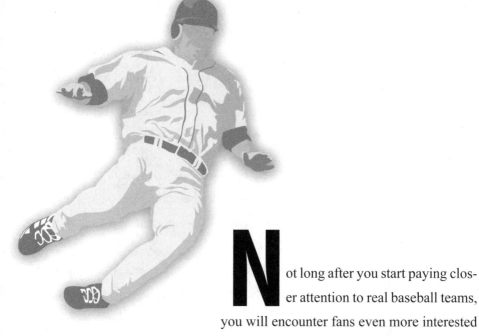

Not long after you start paying closer attention to real baseball teams, you will encounter fans even more interested in the fictional teams they claim to own. On any given day, they will speak of a real player's great game as a personal triumph and another's poor game as an act of sabotage.

This is not the lunatic fringe. There are millions of these fans. And they may soon try to get you to be one of them. They play fantasy baseball and simulation baseball, two hobbies that have allowed many fans to increase their interest in baseball just when they might have abandoned it.

Although these hobbies and the people who enjoy them were once shunned by the baseball establishment, they are now embraced. This is due, in no small part, to the fact that they have successfully infiltrated major league front offices, baseball media, and ballparks everywhere.

Don't let this scare you away. After all, millions of people also watch "reality" TV, take Prozac, or spend countless hours creating online characters in Internet virtual worlds. You too can enjoy playing in a Strat-O-Matic or Rotisserie Baseball league without having to conceal it from your boss, family or girlfriend/boyfriend (although you may want to wait until after the first date to bring it up).

◆ ◆ ◆

"Heroes Are Hard to Find," the band Fleetwood Mac declared on a mid-1970s album of the same name. Lots of baseball fans began thinking that way in the '70s, too, when hometown favorites started scattering through free agency and salary-induced trades.

The start of free agency coincided with an era of labor problems that disrupted seasons. The proliferation of artificial turf and cookie-cutter, multipurpose stadiums added to the feeling that baseball had become artificial. Many regarded (and still regard) the tradition-changing designated hitter rule as sacrilegious. When star players began leaving town to join the highest bidder, favorites looked like mercenaries. When teams began allowing star players to leave, or trading them for untested prospects, rather than pay the salaries set in the new market, owners looked too much like the boss who wouldn't give you a raise.

Feeling disenfranchised and helpless, fans seized what control they could by playing simulation games and launched a revolution that became known as fantasy baseball. This way, the fan decided which players were on his team and what rules they would play by.

Driven by player statistics, both fantasy baseball and simulation games have in turn been key elements in the statistics revolution in baseball, changing the terminology and the way players are judged.

Although simulation games and fantasy baseball are closely related, they are not twins. Time to define *our* terminology:

Baseball Simulation Games

Games such as Strat-O-Matic and APBA simulate the performances of real teams and real players, usually based on completed real seasons. As board games, they accomplish this with player cards and an "activator" (typically dice or a spinner). Computer versions of these games replace the cards and automate the activator with key strokes or mouse clicks.

The best of these games produce quite accurate results for batting, pitching, baserunning and fielding, both individually and league-wide. The fan plays the part of manager, making all in-game strategy decisions (lineups, pitching changes, pinch hitters, stolen bases, intentional walks, etc.). The dice provide an element of chance, but also the math probabilities that allow some players to be rated for a higher average, others for more power or more strikeouts. The games can be played head-to-head or solitaire. Because the games are based on completed seasons, fans can play teams and players from distant historical seasons. At the same time, baseball players are rated individually in these games, allowing fans to divide them in drafts to create fictional teams, thus adding the role of general manager to their resume. By playing in draft "keeper" leagues, simulation gamers become as interested in the current season because that will fuel the statistics for next year's cards and computer ratings.

Fantasy Baseball Leagues

In Rotisserie and other fantasy baseball leagues, the fan is the general manager only—the fan drafts individual players by outbidding others, then gets credit for the players' future achievements in the real games. It's a bit like choosing stocks in the financial markets. There are no in-game strategy decisions and most fantasy leagues do not have to concern themselves with their players' defense, or the lefty-righty balance in their lineups and bullpens the way simulation gamers do. Instead, fantasy leaguers collect players they think will do well in several predetermined batting and pitching categories.

Because fantasy leagues are devoted to today's and tomorrow's statistics, they do not include historical players. Nor do they use real teams—fantasy baseball, by definition, creates fictional teams of individually drafted players. Although simulation gamers can play for money, they usually don't. It's the reverse for fantasy leaguers, who generally bid for major leaguers by the fictional salary they will pay them. This is all about competition—no solitaire play.

Roots of the Games

Fantasy baseball evolved from simulation games. Fantasy's simplicity—no in-game decisions, almost no learning curve to begin play—has made it even more popular and successful than its ancestors.

Simulation games that rate real players date to 1931 and a board game called National Pastime. The first annually published game was All-Star

Baseball (the creation of former Major Leaguer Ethan Allen), which debuted in 1941. The first "full-featured" game—rating players in all phases of the game—was APBA, which enhanced the National Pastime model and debuted in 1951. Strat-O-Matic debuted in 1961, soon became the sales leader, and has remained the board-game leader for two generations. The company estimates that four to five million fans have played its game.

Bill James, the clever author who ignited a national passion for answering questions about player value and baseball strategy through statistics, got his start because he wanted to be better at the simulation board game he played—Ballpark Baseball, a derivative of Strat-O-Matic.

Even more fans play computer games. The most statistically accurate computer simulations are text games, either enhanced conversions of board games, like Strat-O-Matic's PC game, or computer-only games like Diamond Mind. Computer games that combine real-life players and their statistics with arcade-like action—games such as Electronic Arts' *MVP 2005* or the earlier *High Heat*—owe their extreme popularity more to lifelike graphics and action than to statistical accuracy.

The original fantasy game is Rotisserie League Baseball, named for the Manhattan restaurant where its charter members held their first league draft. Rotisserie League Baseball creator Daniel Okrent came up with the idea during a hiatus in his Strat-O-Matic play. Estranged geographically from his Strat partner, Okrent kept the Rotisserie rules simple enough to assure its essential role as a social activity.

That was in 1980. After feature articles in places like *Sports Illustrated* and the now-defunct *Inside Sports*, Rotisserie spawned a national following and an official rule book. By 1989 there were an estimated one million fans playing the game. Since then, the hobby has subdivided faster than some religions and multiplied faster than college football bowl games. Hence the generic "fantasy" baseball label is now worn by an estimated four million fanatics, who can choose different leagues of near-infinite levels of complexity.

How the Games Have Changed "The Game"

Michael Lewis' bestselling book *Moneyball* heightened interest in on-base percentage. Studying how the Oakland A's had remained a consistent pennant contender without an advantageous payroll, Lewis found that the A's had applied statistics to find which areas of on-field performance were undervalued and overvalued in terms of what it cost to acquire the players with those skills. It turned out that a player's ability to draw walks was seriously undervalued.

The economics of the strategy was fresh stuff, but the philosophy of building an offense out of high on-base frequency and power had been successful for generations. Hall of Fame manager Earl Weaver's Baltimore Orioles won four pennants and averaged 97 wins per season from 1969 to 1982 with teams built for the three-run homer: Two walks and a home run would do nicely. His pitching staffs, guided by coach Ray Miller, were legendary for emphasizing first-pitch strikes and avoiding walks.

The *Moneyball* analysis enlightened many, but veteran Strat-O-Matic players had always known that walks were an important part of a team's offense. Each player's Strat-O-Matic card shows his on-base chances—hits and walks—in capital letters. Batters with the most success chances on their cards are the best at creating runs. Pitchers with the least are the best at preventing them. The lowly walk at least adds baserunners and keeps the inning going, increasing the odds that someone batting in the inning will drive in runs.

Very briefly, here's how to play Strat-O-Matic:

You and your opponent choose lineups, including starting pitchers. Now it's Batter vs. Pitcher. Roll three six-sided dice. The first die refers to columns 1, 2 or 3 on the batter's card, or to columns 4, 5, or 6 on the pitcher's card. Add the other two dice to get a result from 2 to 12. Find that number in the correct column and read the result next to it.

Just as at the craps tables in Las Vegas, dice probabilities dictate that a 7 is going to come up on the two added dice much more often than snake eyes or box cars. Johnny Damon has more hits on 6, 7 and 8 rolls than Andruw Jones; Jones has more home run rolls than Damon. Pedro Martinez has many more "strikeout" results than Tom Glavine, but it's a tougher roll to get a home run on Glavine's card than on Martinez' card. The same principle applies to extra-base hits, walks, double-play groundballs, and more.

Some rolls on the pitcher cards refer you to the fielding rating of a defender on his team. Roll again and refer to the fielding chart for players at that position to get the result: out, error or hit.

In Strat-O-Matic's more advanced formats, all players are rated separately for their performance against left- and right-handed opponents. Other options permit results to be adjusted by the ballpark the game is being played in, "clutch" situations and other variables.

Drafting the best player cards, building the best batting orders, and managing the teams through games put simulation gamers ahead of their time in several ways:

- They hold on-base percentage (hits plus walks) in higher regard than ordinary batting average (hits).

- They hold a higher regard still for OPS (on-base plus slugging). Cards filled with success chances *and* extra-base hits—those are the superstars, not the singles-hitting batting champs.

- They recognize that the *components* of a pitcher's earned-run average—walks, hits and home runs allowed (OPS again)—are more revealing than the somewhat useful ERA itself. Strat-O-Matic players anticipating the annual set of new cards (based on the most recently completed season) look at the statistics showing how many walks plus hits a pitcher yielded per inning pitched. A "WHIP" of 1.00 or less is outstanding. Once the WHIP reaches 1.30, that's trouble.

- They learn that there's more to a player's defensive effectiveness than the number of errors he makes. Strat-O-Matic, for example, rates every player from 1 (best) to 5 (disastrous) at each of their defensive positions. Errors influence the grade, but not as much as a player's defensive range. Immobile outfielders who seldom make errors, but who also seldom catch anything that isn't a routine flyball, might be a 3 or even a 4. Players with more errors, but with the talent to consistently turn potential hits into outs will be a 2 or even a 1.

While it took a considerable amount of time, the knowledge and experience gleaned from years of playing games like Strat-O-Matic eventually changed baseball. Some of the biggest names in baseball and sports today used to play: Bob Costas, Jon Miller and Trip Hawkins (creator of the EA Sports video game empire).

As for Rotisserie League Baseball, Strat-O-Matic's influence is clearest in the pitching statistics that the fantasy format uses. The "official" Rotisserie style of fantasy baseball play—there's still an annual book with the rules and the estimated player bid values—is a "5 x 5" fantasy league. That is, teams will compete in five batting-statistics categories and five pitching-statistics categories.

The batting stats are the team's composite batting average, home runs, runs scored, runs batted in, and stolen bases. The pitching stats are wins, saves, innings pitched, composite ERA, and composite WHIP, also called "ratio."

The genius in the design of the original Rotisserie League is that all of the crucial stats can be extracted from the common baseball box score. Everyone had access to the numbers; everyone could play.

The rapid growth of fantasy baseball has revolutionized baseball information:

● Because fantasy gamers are looking for a competitive edge, they read voraciously. To meet this demand, magazines, newspapers, web sites, and numerous books are full of individual player stats, forecasts, scouting reports, and rankings.

● Because fantasy gamers only get credit for stats their players achieve, information on who is playing is precious. Newspapers and web sites

Very briefly, here's how to play Rotisserie League Baseball:

Each gamer has a salary cap. It must be distributed to accumulate a roster that will do well in as many of the league's statistical categories as possible. Each team will get points depending on how well it ranks vis-à-vis the other teams in each statistical category.

Your group meets to draft players by bidding your fictional dollars, $280 per team for a league of drafted National League players. You're going to need twenty-five players, so that's an average just over $11 per man. If you pay $38 for Albert Pujols (his projected value before the 2006 season began), you're going to have to surround him with less talent. You might spend less on pitching, or you might gamble that you can find the low-priced backup outfielder who is going to be the next surprise star.

Once your team is complete, you monitor each player's performance. Throughout the season, you make trades or replace unproductive players with others who are free agents (owned by no other teams). Rotisserie teams seldom have the luxury of standing pat. A real player gets hurt and he's worth nothing to you. Another gets traded to a team where he will have a smaller role and he's no longer worth what you paid for him. Manipulating your roster resembles playing the stock market: Can you buy low (before a player gets hot) and sell high (when a player's peak is over)?

Finally, all teams are ranked in each category and points are assigned accordingly. In a ten-team league, for example, 10 points are given to the top-ranked team in each category, 9 to the next best, etc. The team with the most points wins the pennant.

now faithfully carry all player-transaction information—who has been traded, demoted to the minors, or promoted. If a player is benched or injured, we now almost always hear how long the player is expected to be out of the lineup and who will replace him, and how the dominoes will fall in the batting order or the pitching rotation.

● Because competitive fantasy gamers need to be the first to grab hot young talent before it becomes too familiar and too expensive, baseball fans now have access to more information about minor-league prospects and the college/high school players expected to be drafted by major league teams each spring.

● It's now common to see "fantasy-impact" reports with the Internet site reports on almost every major league game.

The chief byproduct of baseball simulation games and fantasy baseball is the deeper interest they create in the real sport. Most regular fans are homers—they know much about their hometown team, little about any others. Simulation and fantasy gamers are talent scouts—they research and follow the fortunes of every major league team and their farm teams. Late season games between also-ran teams are of great interest to simulation and fantasy gamers—their drafted players appear in those box scores. Similarly, a late-inning at-bat by, say, Adam Dunn in a 9-1 game is of great interest to the "owners" of Dunn and the pitcher facing him, and of some interest to all the other franchise owners in the league.

These fans support baseball rabidly. They buy tickets to Spring Training games as well as regular season games. They buy memorabilia, board and video games, and other products that pay royalties to players and leagues. They speak about the game with passion few other fans can equal.

THE LAST FRONTIER
Fielding Stats Still Confound Researchers

There's no dispute that Willie Mays had one of the strongest, most accurate throwing arms of any outfielder in history. A beer commercial exalting Mays once touted the "hundreds of runners he threw out at home plate." Nice legend, but like most others, exaggerated.

In his 22 seasons as an outfielder, Mays threw out 195 men—at all bases combined. He led the National League in outfield assists exactly once. The true testimony to Mays' throwing skill is not how many men he threw out, but how many he never had the chance to throw out. Soon after Mays' arrival in the major leagues, opposing baserunners knew not to challenge him. They tried to take the extra base against Mays only when it was a sure thing—or so they thought.

Fielding remains a frustrating area of baseball analysis after so much illumination elsewhere on the diamond. Batting and pitching remain topics of fertile debate, but the statistics used to evaluate them have mostly been demystified. So much of what happens on the baseball field is decided by the pitcher and batter that we have much more data to work with and many more eager researchers to translate it. By comparison, fielding evaluations are trapped in a Bermuda Triangle of legend, perception and woefully inadequate statistics.

For the most part, fielding skill has been measured by errors, total chances (errors + putouts + assists), and fielding percentage ((putouts + assists) / total chances).

Errors are supposed to tell us how adept (or clumsy) a fielder is—except that they don't. Some fielders make more errors because their other skills—speed, agility, instincts, desire—get them to far more balls. They are assigned errors because they get their gloves on balls that other fielders would wave by, instead of letting them be scored as hits.

Total chances, expressed as total chances per game, is less judgmental about errors and therefore is supposed to be an improvement, at least to express a defender's range, if not his sure-handedness. But a superior second baseman's skill might be disguised on a team with a disproportionate amount of flyball pitchers, or strikeout pitchers. He will also get fewer opportunities—and therefore fewer chances—if his pitching staff is disproportionately left-handed. Lefty pitchers face 75-85% right-handed hitters, whose ground-balls go mostly to the shortstop and third baseman. It takes considerably more analysis to isolate these and similar factors.

Fielding percentage is supposed to account for all this. The extra errors would be absorbed by the many more chances successfully handled. This works a little better, but not well enough. A truly bad fielding percentage is revealing, but a spectacular fielding percentage is not. It is possible for a lead-footed, unambitious outfielder to play a whole season with zero, or very few errors, while softly hit balls consistently fall in front of him and harder-hit drives sail to his left and right, and over his head. It's not only possible—it happens.

Even then, the variables are cloudy. Which of these left- and right-handed pitchers allow fewer balls to be pulled? Ballparks influence fielding too. Bounces behave differently on turf and grass and on better-maintained infields or in certain weather conditions. Altitude, humidity, sun and wind direction affect the difficulty in tracking flyballs. And how do we measure how hard the balls were hit?

The chemistry is murkier still when evaluating throwing skill. For outfielders, the throwing statistic is assists—the men they threw out on the bases. That's a notoriously deceiving stat—often, players well-known for their weak arms will be among the league leaders in assists. Opposing runners attempt the extra base against them much more often, and take riskier chances. The weak-armed outfielder has many more opportunities for assists than the rifle-armed outfielder who freezes baserunners.

Simple or complex, the traditional evaluation systems break down. A half dozen competing systems to evaluate fielders offer little more than curiosity value because they so radically disagree with each other. If a fielder is a savior in one system and a liability in another, both systems may be suspect. If they also disagree with the circumstantial evidence—daily "web gem" highlight shows and Gold Glove awards voted on by managers and coaches—then we either have a bright new light or rubbish. As of now, we don't know which.

There are a few things that can be said confidently about defense:

- Errors decline and fielding averages go up with every generation of play.

  The various reasons include the size and design of baseball gloves, the condition of playing surfaces, better coaching/positioning, and the leniency of modern official scorers. Herman Long, considered a good shortstop, made 117 errors in 1889. Honus Wagner, considered one of the greatest shortstops ever, made 49-60 errors every year from 1903-1910. When shortstop Edgar Renteria made 30 errors in 2005, he was accused of sabotaging the Boston Red Sox' pennant hopes and was traded after the season for a minor leaguer. Six regular shortstops made fewer than 10 errors in 2006.

- The steady shrinkage in errors means that now the statistical difference between a league leader and a middle-of-the-pack defender looks miniscule.

  Gold Glove winner Mark Teixeira made the fewest errors (4) and had the highest fielding percentage (.997) of all who played at least 115 games at first base in 2006. The worst offender in Teixeira's

American League was Toronto's Lyle Overbay, who made all of 9 errors and fielded .994. At shortstop, where the percentages are more extreme, 15 regulars fielded between .970 and .980.

● The Gold Glove awards consistently reward the spectacularly great fielders, but sometimes the voting is more suspect than the municipal elections in Chicago.

Torii Hunter, Andruw Jones and Ichiro Suzuki reliably get the gold, as did Ozzie Smith and Brooks Robinson. But shaky right fielder Bobby Abreu got his first Gold Glove in 2005. Rafael Palmeiro got one in 1999 after playing only 28 games at first base and serving as the designated hitter in 128 games.

● Even without good defensive statistics, we understand enough about pitching to know that defense is a distant second to pitching in run prevention. Even so, defense can make or break big-league careers. Countless hot prospects have had very short careers after their defense was found wanting, especially at the "up-the-middle" positions (catcher, second base, shortstop, center field). Countless others have been converted from one of these positions to a corner infield or outfield spot.

Lost-cause fielders have played in the big leagues. But usually they haven't played for long unless they have the prodigious power of Harmon Killebrew or Dick Stuart.

◆ ◆ ◆

With no superior rating system and no consensus about how to evaluate defense statistically, a new book has hit on the novel idea of presenting as much data as possible. In this way, *The Fielding Bible* seeks to provide an accounting of each fielder's strengths and weaknesses, relative to the skill of the average player in a given position through an innovative plus/minus system. Rather than a single rating built on debatable assumption, *The Fielding Bible* presents a composite view of each player.

In the introduction to John Dewan's book, Bill James explains:

> *We are trying to ask specific questions about the player's defensive skills, so that, in time, we can create enough of an image of the player's defense that we will be able to "see" intuitively what we have left out. How well does this second baseman turn the double play? How well does that third baseman field a bunt? How well does that shortstop go to his left? How well does he go to his right? ...It is my belief that the simple accumulation of facts, in time, will help us to understand more than we now understand.*

The Fielding Bible does this—and more—for each player and each team. The basic stats (e.g. putouts, assists, errors, fielding percentage) appear next to unique data: how each first and third baseman does on bunts; how each middle infielder does on double plays; how all infielders do on balls to their left, right and "straight on;" how strong outfielders' arms are (both in throwing runners out and preventing advances).

By providing a three-year data set for each player, we begin to see certain patterns about a player's assets and his deficiencies.

The team profile includes a visual representation of where on the diamond all hits landed—balls down the line, between infielders, in front of outfielders, over outfielders, in the gaps, off the walls, over the walls. Looking at Boston, for example, we can see the influence of Fenway Park—significantly more balls were hit off the left field wall than the league average. We also can see the influence of suspect Sox left fielder Manny Ramirez—significantly more hits down the left field line and in the left field gap.

The data is the product of analyzing video of every play of the season. So the *Fielding Bible*'s own catch-all stat, a plus/minus system of "expected outs," might be subject to challenge and debate, but it has the virtue of transparency—*The Fielding Bible* supplies the ammunition to attack (or support) any of its findings.

Best of all, *The Fielding Bible* is forthright about what we do not yet understand, and therefore remarkably free of dubious assertions like how many hundreds of men Andruw Jones has thrown out at home plate.

WAIT TILL NEXT YEAR

The Quest to Understand
the Game Continues

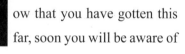

ow that you have gotten this far, soon you will be aware of other statistics—some thought-provoking, some thoughtless. We are going to draw your attention to several statistics that have gained momentum in recent years—enough so that you might want to add them to your vocabulary once you have become comfortable with the other statistics in this book.

But first, we offer this preface.

Curiosity about baseball statistics has been widening and deepening each year. More people are interested and they want to know more than ever before. Like scientific research, a discovery advances the quest for truth but doesn't end it. If anything, the discovery expands the possibilities for new research, exposing passageways to be explored.

That said, sometimes the supply of new statistics exceeds the demand.

Wider and deeper databases, and new tools to analyze them, make research more plentiful. But just because we *can* track certain things, doesn't necessarily mean we *should*. Consider this item that a wire service sent across the country in late April 2006:

> *The New York Yankees joined the 1992 Toronto Blue Jays and 2003 Seattle Mariners as the only teams since 1976 to win their first eight day games. Seattle started 17-0 in the daylight that year. The Yankees' next day game is today at home against the Blue Jays.*

Wow. Drop everything to make it to the stadium today or risk missing the extension—or tragic end—to that streak of daytime wins. Talk about drama. Let's not mention that at this point the Yankees have played four straight *night* games and, as usual, more night games than day games. I mean, if the Yankees can win just *nine more* consecutive day games—check back with us in June on that one—they'll be just the second team since way back in 2003 to win at least 17 day games in a row.

This sort of statistical noise isn't even worthy of the term trivia. Unfortunately, the search for the useful can be distorted by a cacophony of statistical irrelevance. Whether researching statistics or studying them, consider this:

● **Who cares?** A good question to ask before writing, computing, researching, or experimenting on anything.

- **Cause and effect.** Are two or more simultaneous events linked by anything more than coincidence? If we could prove that the manufacture of baseballs has changed at the same time that more home runs are being hit, would that prove the ball is the cause? Not unless we could isolate it from other changes like the strike zone, pitching practices, and weather.

- **Selective memory.** Often used to advocate a player for the Hall of Fame, this technique finds a stat or two that favors the player, then argues, "Everyone else who has this many of that" is in the Hall of Fame—ignoring that everyone else also has a lot more of the other things missing from the first player's game. A variation on this theme: Combine a couple of stats that favor the player with a couple that are mediocre and declare, "My man is one of only 12 players in history to achieve XX home runs, XX doubles, XX walks and XX stolen bases," in the hopes that the whole will look greater than the sum of the parts. Invariably, none of the thresholds achieved is Hall-worthy.

- **Lowest-common denominator.** Another Hall of Fame argument: "He has more home runs (or hits, or wins, or saves, etc.) than anyone not in the Hall of Fame." If that was reason enough to elect someone to the Hall, then as soon as that was done, the next guy on the list would have to get in, and the one after him, and on and on until *every* player was in the Hall.

Flaws like these generally betray the presenter's bias. Advocacy has its own merits, but it's the natural predator of open-minded research.

Researchers like Bill James, John Dewan, the folks at Baseball Prospectus, and a few others have earned substantial and sustained followings by inviting others along on their pursuit of understanding. The pursuit usually starts by keeping in perspective the above points and always asking: Is this information actually helpful?

◆ ◆ ◆

Some of the statistics developed by the innovative researchers mentioned above have become widely quoted, though not so widely that you will see them posted on scoreboards or cited on baseball broadcasts. These are complicated enough that they are resistant to the abbreviation necessary in those places. But if you continue to pursue your curiosity about baseball statistics, you will soon encounter these terms:

Runs Created

James developed this measure long ago to combine all of the major elements of a batter's offensive performance. *The Bill James Handbook* describes Runs Created this way: "an estimate of the number of a team's runs which are created by each individual hitter." That is followed by a page and a half describing the formula and how to tweak it. To simplify: It's the number of times a hitter gets on base (minus his times caught stealing and double-play groundouts) multiplied by the effect of his hits, walks and sacrifices to advance other runners, all divided by his plate appearances. The result is a powerful number that can also be tweaked to show how often a team full of such offensive players would score.

Win Shares

In 2002, Bill James and Jim Henzler published a groundbreaking volume that presents in a single number the contribution made by any player—batter or pitcher—to his team's wins and includes each player's offensive and defensive roles in that rating. The "short-form method" to calculate Win Shares is a 13-step process. The long-form method is…a book. So Win Shares is beyond our ability to do it justice here. But James describes Win Shares as "Wins Created" except that there are three "shares" to each win. Even if the math is more than you want, the book is a treasure for all who want to delve into the history of baseball. James has calculated and distributed Win Shares to the players on every major league team in baseball from 1876 to 2001. Then he created more lists by recombining all the players by position and by era. The book has lots of numbers, but it has fascinating essays too.

VORP (Value Over Replacement Level)

We're not sure why the folks at Baseball Prospectus didn't call it Value Over Replacement Player if they were going to use the "P" instead of the incompatible "L" in the acronym, because "player" works just fine to describe VORP. Regardless, this stat measures how much better a player's performance was than the typical bench player at his position. Many previous statistical measures compare performance to the average player, but VORP recognizes that if a player gets hurt, or otherwise misses time, his replacement is not going to be the average player—he's going to be somebody barely above minor-league level.

VORP is a handy number to have to compare value between two or more players. If you are a big-league general manager considering a trade,

VORP can compare your left fielder's relative worth to that of the other team's pitcher. Or you can use the VORP ratings for all left fielders to find out how difficult it will be to get a comparable replacement. If you are a simulation gamer or fantasy player, you can use VORP to see which players give you the widest competitive edge at their positions.

PECOTA (Player Empirical Comparison and Optimization Test Algorithm)

Runs Created, Win Shares, and VORP all provide clues about future value, but they measure *past* performance. PECOTA (the acronym is the last name of a former big-league utility infielder) is a forecasting system, not terribly unlike the weather forecasts that tell you there's a 25% chance of rain. PECOTA takes a player's past performance, factors his age, his position, his ballpark, and much more, and then compares him to every other player since 1949 to find the best matches. This is used to project the percentage likelihood that the current player will have a breakout performance, mere improvement, normal "attrition," or a collapse in the forthcoming season.

Yes, it takes a computer to calculate PECOTA. And the system is proprietary at Baseball Prospectus, so you can't monkey around with it. But if you are a simulation-game or fantasy-league general manager, it might be comforting for you to know that the real GMs take PECOTA seriously.

◆ ◆ ◆

Runs Created, Win Shares and VORP have something in common besides being more complex than box scores. They are the most credible explorations so far in what might be called the search for the Holy Grail of baseball statistics: The single number that will express a player's full value.

All three of these measures—PECOTA, too—are products of modern "sabermetrics," the term derived from SABR, the acronym for the Society for American Baseball Research. SABR members explore many research topics, including biographies and off-the-field material, but the national non-profit organization is best known for its sabermetricians, who are devoted to statistical analysis.

Someday, one of them is going to come up with the GRAIL (General Rating and Impact Level) stat. GRAIL will be universally accepted as the measure that so reliably compares players of any era to each other and accurately weighs their impact on winning that it will be used to balance trades, determine salaries, set gambling odds, and settle all sports-bar debates.

A player's GRAIL will be better known than his jersey number. Hall of Fame voting will be a formality. Talk shows will stick to football.

Of course, even *if* a GRAIL stat were possible, who would want to give up all the debate, study, intrigue and excitement statistics bring to the new ballgame?

APPENDIX
Statistical Resources

"You could look it up," Hall of Fame Manager Casey Stengel once observed.

I looked up a lot as I wrote this book. My constant companions included these mainstays of statistical information.

In the interest of full disclosure, some of the books listed here were published by ACTA Sports, which also published this book. What can I say? This is a book about statistics, and they're a statistics publisher. You don't go to a podiatrist when you need brain surgery.

The Bill James Handbook (ACTA Sports)

This annual is the handiest reference for finding the performance of every current player, both last year and for his big-league career. It includes league and team-by-team stats, and league leaders. If all you want is that basic information, this is your book. But there is so much more in the *Handbook* that is difficult or impossible to find elsewhere: data on each manager's tactics, the influence of each ballpark, detailed fielding data, and unique leader boards such as "tough saves." It also contains such Bill James specialties as Runs Created, Win Shares, hitter projections and career assessments. Oh, and then there's the baserunning analysis, and the Fielding Bible Awards, and…

The 2006 ESPN Baseball Encylopedia, edited by Pete Palmer and Gary Gillette (Sterling Publishing Co.)

Every baseball library needs an up-to-date encyclopedia. This particular one is updated the most often. Nearly 1,300 of its 1,700-plus pages are devoted to the year-by-year and career statistics (traditional and Sabermetric) of every player in major league history. This is the best source for looking up former players or for comparing current players to past. The book has many other virtues, such as detailed breakdowns on historic performances (e.g. Joe DiMaggio's day-by-day 56-game hitting streak) and single-season and career leaders in a remarkable number of categories, including pre-1900 performances. There's never been so much information in one place at such an affordable price. There's never been so much information in one place, period.

The Sports Encylopedia: Baseball 2006, by David S. Neft, Richard M. Cohen & Michael L.Neft (St. Martin's Griffin)

Updated annually, this is the most comprehensive collection of baseball history presented one season at a time. The detail on every season from 1901 to 2005, including complete rosters for each team, is unmatched by any other printed source. If you want to check out, say, the 1941 season (or any other single season), this is the first place to go. This volume's 800-plus pages make it a bit handier for speed-checking of single-season, career leaders and award winners, especially if you don't want them infiltrated by pre-1900 performances.

www.baseball-almanac.com

The Baseball Almanac online has a rich supply of contemporary and historic information—statistics, lists (e.g. all no-hitters or four-home-run games), accounts of how the game has evolved (e.g. rules, uniforms), notable quotations and much more.

www.baseball-reference.com

Baseball Reference online is organized more like an encyclopedia, combining the player-by-player comprehensiveness of the printed *ESPN Encylopedia* and the team-by-team comprehensiveness of *The Sports Encyclopedia*. It's a reference for much more, including unique features such as finding any player's most statistically comparable players in history.

www.retrosheet.org

The ".org" extension is significant: The generous work by David Smith and his band of volunteers is the foundation for many other baseball research projects, from books to websites to game ratings. Retrosheet's mission is to collect and collate play-by-play data on every major league game ever played. After a generation of creativity and diligence, it is getting close to its goal. That yields a rich supply of basic information (you can even look up the box score of almost any game) and a database that allows advanced users to answer such questions as: How did Ted Williams do against left-handed pitching for his career (or, say, against Whitey Ford)?

OTHER STATISTICAL SOURCES

There are countless options, online and in print, but these are staples.

Society for American Baseball Research (www.sabr.org)

This non-profit organization is devoted to baseball research (statistics, biographies, players/non-players, all eras, you name it). Its active online listserve (SABR-L) is the hangout for many of the most knowledgeable baseball fans. Newspaper writers, TV producers, book authors, and more go there for answers. Original research appears here all the time, and then comes out of the mouths of baseball announcers. Your nominal paid membership to SABR also gets you several annual print publications and online access to historical newspapers. It's a treasure trove of baseball information. Some of it is fun and easy (a list of all catchers who have caught more than one no-hitter). Some is more advanced (the earned-run averages of the pitchers who are caught by certain catchers). Some of it is for people who have fun with exponents and square roots.

The Sporting News Baseball Guide and *Baseball Register*

Two annuals with vast amounts of data. The *Guide* is a review of the past season, plus historic data on pennant winners, award winners, and more. The *Register* is the career-long, year-by-year statistics of every current player, including minor league performances.

Online sources updated regularly:

www.mlb.com, www.espn.com, www.foxsports.com, www.si.com, www.sportingnews.com, www.usatoday.com.

These sites, among others, for Major League Baseball, ESPN, Fox Sports, *Sports Illustrated, The Sporting News* and *USA Today* are ideal for tracking the current season beyond the home team—with news, scores, stats and more. Your choice depends on your preference for how the data is presented, how far back it is archived, how interested you are in fantasy baseball, and how annoyed you are by how espn.com obliterates its superior information with incessant pop-up ads.

OTHER SOURCES RELEVANT TO THIS BOOK:

Baseball: The Biographical Encylopedia (Total/Sports Illustrated)

Published in 2000, this compilation of 2,000 compact biographies remains a vital reference for anyone writing about historically significant players.

The Fielding Bible by John Dewan and Baseball Info Solutions (ACTA Sports)

Published in 2006, this book lives up to its billing as "breakthrough analysis of Major League Baseball defense—by team and player." Never has defense been so thoroughly considered and documented. This is uniquely valuable because defensive skill is the one major area of baseball that has mostly eluded credible statistical analysis. Until now, that is.

Rotisserie League Baseball: The Official Rule Book and Guide (published and edited by John Benson)

This contains everything you need to know to play Rotisserie League Baseball: how to organize or join a league, how to build winning teams, and the salaries (plus scouting reports) for hundreds of players. It is updated annually.

Strat-O-Matic Fanatics: The Unlikely Success Story of a Game That Became an American Passion by Glenn Guzzo (ACTA Sports)

This book tells the story behind Strat-O-Matic's creation, popularity and survival against the odds that overwhelmed many of its contemporary competitors. And it documents how this hobby inspired the baseball-statistics revolution we enjoy today.

Baseball Prospectus (Penguin Group)

This book provides analyses of the top players in each organization with objective data, insightful commentary, and irreverent humor. Its proprietary projections system "PECOTA" makes this book unique.

Ron Shandler's Baseball Forecaster (Shandler Enterprises, LLC)

A staple in the fantasy baseball world, this book offers projections based on player performance with analytical support to back up those projections.

The Hardball Times Baseball Annual by The Hardball Times writers (ACTA Sports)

This analysis of the entire season even includes a breakdown of the postseason and World Series, but still comes out before the end of November. It also contains timely guest essays from some of the brightest minds in baseball. The Hardball Times is a baseball think tank of writers who create provocative, insightful and entertaining baseball analyses, as well as produce their own unique statistics, graphs and essays. Their website, www.hardballtimes.com is updated daily throughout the year on all things baseball.

Other Books from ACTA Sports

HOW BILL JAMES CHANGED OUR VIEW OF BASEBALL
by Colleagues, Critics, Competitors and Just Plain Fans
edited by Gregory F. Augustine Pierce

In this collection of twelve essays by some of the sharpest minds in baseball, the contributors show how Bill James has changed the way they think about a lot of things, including baseball. 144-page hardcover, $14.95

THE BILL JAMES HANDBOOK
by Bill James and Baseball Info Solutions

Always the first and certainly the best of the annual baseball statistical analysis books. It contains all the lifetime stats from all the players who played Major League Baseball the previous season. 466-page paperback, $21.95

THE HARDBALL TIMES BASEBALL ANNUAL
Edited by Dave Studenmund

A comprehensive analysis of the entire previous season from the first pitch to the last out, including a review of the playoffs and the World Series. Written by the think tank of baseball writers at the popular website www.hardballtimes.com. 350-page paperback, $19.95

JOHN DEWAN'S FIELDING BIBLE
by John Dewan

The breakthrough analysis of baseball defense that is revolutionizing how people think about fielding statistics. Includes major contributions from Bill James and Baseball Info Solutions. 241-page paperback, $19.95

THE LIFE OF LOU GEHRIG
Told by a Fan
by Sara Kaden Brunsvold

This complete biography looks at the legendary New York Yankee first baseman from the point of view of a fan, revealing what Gehrig and his legacy have meant to her and other baseball fans. 252-page paperback, $14.95

Available from booksellers or call 800-397-2282
www.actasports.com

Other Books from ACTA Sports

BEHIND-THE-SCENES BASEBALL
Real-Life Applications of Statistical Analysis Actually Used by Major League Teams...and Other Stories from the Inside
by Doug Decatur

An insider's look into why, when and how analytical managers and GMs use the practical application of baseball statistics to make key decisions in a game and over a season. Includes the popular "GM IQ Test." 311-page paperback, $14.95

STRAT-O-MATIC FANATICS
The Unlikely Success Story of a Game
That Became an American Passion
by Glenn Guzzo

The award-winning book about the creation—and re-creation—of America's most popular sports board game ever. Tells the story of Hal Richman, who beat the odds and invented a game that has been played by thousands of baseball fans for over forty years. 320-page paperback, $14.95

DIAMOND PRESENCE
Twelve Stories of Finding God at the Old Ball Park
edited by Gregory F. Augustine Pierce

A collection of true stories in which the authors relate how they came to feel the presence of God while enjoying the great American pastime as players, coaches, parents, children, or just plain fans. 175-page hardcover, $17.95

THE BALLGAME OF LIFE
Lessons for Parents and Coaches of Young Baseball Players
by David Allen Smith and Joseph Aversa, Jr.
with a Foreword by Peter Gammons

A book for parents and coaches who love baseball and want to be involved in encouraging children to learn and enjoy it. Contains practical advice, *true stories about youth baseball*, and *"Life Skills Learning Drills."* 126-page paperback, $9.95

Available from booksellers or call 800-397-2282
www.actasports.com

More praise for *The New Ballgame*

Baseball has needed a Stats 101 class for a long time. This book is required reading for anyone new to baseball's numbers.
—Alan Schwarz, senior writer for *Baseball America*

Statistics do not just provide a droll chronicle of baseball's play-by-play. **The New Ballgame** shows how they provide the "color" to understanding the game and enrich the experience of being a fan.
—Ron Shandler, author, *Baseball Forecaster*, and publisher, BaseballHQ.com

As Glenn Guzzo says in this insightful survey, "statistics are the language of baseball." Guzzo doesn't just define baseball stats, he shows how they're used at the ballpark and on television. He tells you how to score a game and how to read a box score. And his review of "Why Baseball Arguments Never Die" is especially useful for interpreting the language of baseball. Every beginning baseball fan will find this book useful, and I can think of a number of "veteran" fans I'd like to give it to, as well.
—Dave Studenmund, editor of *The Hardball Times Baseball Annual*

Glenn Guzzo draws from both recent events and the vastness of baseball history to introduce readers to basic baseball stats, as well as a few new-fangled ones. Even if you already know your way around a box score, Guzzo's prose and his choices of examples will make this a fun read.
—John Zajc, Executive Director, Society for American Baseball Research